OUT OF
THE
WRECK

I RISE

OUT OF THE WRECK I RISE

A LITERARY COMPANION TO RECOVERY

Neil Steinberg and Sara Bader

The University of Chicago Press   CHICAGO AND LONDON

The University of Chicago Press, Chicago 60637 | The University of Chicago Press, Ltd., London | © 2016 by Neil Steinberg and Sara Bader | All rights reserved. Published 2016. | Paperback edition 2018.
Printed in the United States of America

27 26 25 24 23 22 21 20 19 18   7 8 9 10 11

ISBN-13: 978-0-226-14013-1 (cloth)
ISBN-13: 978-0-226-52874-8 (paper)
ISBN-13: 978-0-226-14027-8 (e-book)
DOI: 10.7208/chicago/9780226140278.001.0001

Library of Congress Cataloging-in-Publication Data
Names: Steinberg, Neil, compiler. | Bader, Sara, compiler.
Title: Out of the wreck I rise : a literary companion to recovery /
Neil Steinberg and Sara Bader.
Description: Chicago ; London : The University of Chicago Press, 2016. |
Includes bibliographical references and index.
Identifiers: LCCN 2015042766 | ISBN 9780226140131 (cloth : alk. paper) |
ISBN 9780226140278 (e-book)
Subjects: LCSH : Alcoholism—Quotations, maxims, etc. | Alcoholism—
Psychological aspects—Quotations, maxims, etc. | Alcoholism—Treatment—
Quotations, maxims, etc. | Alcoholism—Miscellanea.
Classification: LCC HV5072.S9145 2016 | DDC 362.292—dc23
LC record available at http://lccn.loc.gov/2015042766

♾ This paper meets the requirements of ANSI/NISO Z39.48-1992 (Permanence of Paper).

CONTENTS

WHY PUT IT OFF?

It's the hardest thing you'll ever do. Subduing alcoholism or over-coming some other addiction pits you not only against a power-ful chemical craving—your mind screams for the stuff—but also against strong social pressure. Everyone does it. All your friends do it. You've always done it, for years. It's always been fun—well, almost always. Okay, not always fun, and not everybody does it. Still, your life revolves around it. It is who you *are*.

And now you have to stop, to give it up somehow. Maybe you even want to. It's time. You just know. More likely you have to. Something terrible has happened: the law looms; you're about to lose your job; your wife walked out; your husband is going to divorce you; your body is breaking down. You don't want to stop, but there's no choice.

You turn for help—and almost everyone needs help. You can't do it alone; it's hard enough to do with help. Nearly impossible, or so it seems, especially at first. But help helps. You plunge into the fluorescent-lit world of rehab centers, support groups, thera-pists, and, of course, AA—Alcoholics Anonymous—the bul-wark of recovery, that in-every-city, around-the-clock, all-day, everyday, always-there, free system of mutual support from your fellow sufferers.

For millions of people that works. They get sober, experience some kind of spiritual awakening, find fellowship, and turn their lives around.

But for many, that isn't enough. What seems to be working so well for those in AA isn't working for them. The familiar mottos — One Day at a Time, Easy Does It, Fake It until You Make It — might help overcome the immediate challenge of the next few hours and days, but they require something else. Something uniquely powerful that can offer clarity amid the confusion, provisions for the steep climb ahead.

Fortunately, assistance is out there, waiting, concealed within the poetry of the past, tucked away in philosophy, and hiding in plain sight in popular culture. Because one central truth of addiction is that, as lonely as you feel, you are not, in fact, alone. Not only are millions struggling right now with the same problem you are facing, but millions more have struggled with it over the centuries. Among them, writers and philosophers, poets and playwrights, who have thought and written about this fight for thousands of years.

"If you had a sty," the Roman writer Horace counsels his friend Lollius Maximus three decades before the birth of Jesus, "you'd be in a hurry to cure it; if the sickness is in your soul, why put it off?" He continues:

> Get yourself going and you'll be halfway there;
> Dare to be wise; get started. The man who puts off
> The time to start living right is like the hayseed
> Who wants to cross the river and so he sits there
> Waiting for the river to run out of water,
> And the river flows by, and it flows on by, forever.

That is the purpose of this book: to get you started toward living right, toward a better life you might not even realize is out there. Or if you have already stepped onto the bridge, to keep you focused and inspired, to fortify your besieged spirit and feed your hungry and battered mind something substantial. To help you realize that while addiction can seem romantic, recovery is the path of the hero.

This collection can be shared with family and friends to help them understand what you are going through, that this isn't some weakness that you foolishly embraced and refuse to abandon, but a sickness that has seized you, a trap you've fallen into and are now trying to climb out of—with their help, if possible, without it, if necessary.

As for spiritual rebirth, while that does happen for some, becoming sober does not require divine intervention. Or as Dante writes in *Purgatorio*, the middle book of his *Divine Comedy*: "Let us posit as a given: every love that's kindled in you arises necessarily. Still, the power to constrain it lies with you."

Faith and human will are not at odds. Legions credit God for helping them stay sober, others embrace the idea behind Dante's quote. There is no need to weigh the two and pick one—in the fight against addiction, use whatever works. For some people, that's God or a "higher power," however it's defined; for others, it's the strength Dante finds inherent in each individual. Many alternate between the two, combining prayer and personal determination. Dante's point is, you may not be able to control what you yearn for, but you can decide what to do about your troublesome desires—that is, if you try and you keep at it and you have help.

We believe that poetry helps. We believe that philosophy helps. Seeing your thoughts and experiences reflected on the page can offer epiphany and validation. "Other people's words," writes British novelist Zadie Smith, "are the bridge you use to cross from where you were to wherever you're going."

True sentiments expressed in plain language embroider the long, often-mundane recovery process and give us something to grab onto. They accompany us on our journey and are always available when we need them. Quotes, according to Geoffrey O'Brien, editor of *Bartlett's Familiar Quotations*, "are the dangling threads that memory can latch onto when everything else goes blank."

The right phrase can act as a talisman. For those yearning for their days of blissful ignorance, before this problem was laid out in such stark form, it can be a balm to remember a line from Sarah McLachlan's essential anthem, "Fallen" — "Better I should know." Four common words, none poetic or profound, but strung together they form a blunt, unambiguous statement, a shield to deflect the regret and sorrow of losing your substance-abusing life. Yes, the truth is ugly. Yes, you messed up. The present course is arduous. Success, uncertain. Still, better you should know.

Given the difficulty of long-term sobriety—the siren call always tries to lure you back—why not enlist the finest thinkers and writers of all time as your helpers and guides? The idea of sponsorship lies at the core of AA's philosophy. A sponsor — your ally, instructor, teacher, friend—leads the way through the psychological labyrinth of recovery. Why not ask Virgil to be one of your trusted sponsors? Dante conjured him up as a guide through hell—so can you. "Yield not to evils," Virgil writes in *The Aeneid*. "But go forth all the bolder to face them."

That's a plan.

This book's title, *Out of the Wreck I Rise*, comes from Robert Browning's poem "Ixion," about a mythological king bound to a wheel in hell, "whirling forever in torment." He remembers his former glory — "For the past was dream: now that the dreamers awake"—then contemplates the struggle for redemption, hope kindling even "from the tears and sweat and blood of his torment." He urges action instead of despair, effort instead of resignation:

> Strive, my kind, though strife endure through endless
>   obstruction,
> Stage after stage, each rise marred by as certain a fall!

Browning reminds us that with persistence and effort you can do it. Each fall, though perhaps certain, is not final. Setbacks will occur and be overcome. Every day, countless people who have wrecked their lives through one addiction or another perform the hard work of putting those lives back together and keeping them that way. Whatever abyss you have fallen into, there is a pathway back to the living world.

This book attempts to walk the reader along the route from the hell of addiction to the frequent bliss of recovery, each chapter beginning with commentary followed by relevant quotes. The book draws on the works of writers from Seneca to Shakespeare to David Foster Wallace and includes the voices of popular figures, including Billie Holiday, Keith Richards, and Patti Smith. Notorious drinkers—John Cheever, Charles Bukowski, Ernest Hemingway, Eugene O'Neill, and Raymond Carver, among others—share dearly paid-for wisdom. Most appear once or twice. Certain writers return from time to time—Samuel Johnson, Jack London, Domenica Ruta—to take you along on their arduous journeys. And sometimes a thought that originally wasn't referring to addiction, from an author who didn't struggle with substance abuse, also serves as a guide. When Edith Wharton wrote that she "generally behaved myself—a sensation still having the charm of novelty," she was fourteen and might never have tasted alcohol. Yet the remark captures the deceptive temporary giddiness of early sobriety. When Saul Bellow writes that "recovery is possible" in *Seize the Day*, he isn't talking specifically about addiction or referring to himself. Just as in the real world, addicts and nonaddicts work together to treat this illness, so the insights of the affected and unaffected, braided together, form a stronger rope to toss to those treading the icy chop of addiction.

These quotations not only inspire individually but are also fitted together to form a mosaic, creating a narrative of how recovery unfolds. Some we discovered in familiar classics, novels, plays, memoirs, and popular culture, but we also mined deeper into obscure letter collections, out-of-print diaries, and forgotten editions. Sources for every excerpt are listed at the back of the book for those wishing to read these thoughts in context or to further explore the works of a particular author. This collection serves as a reminder that countless men and women have blazed this painful path, leaving behind directions and warnings, markers and encouragement, a useful map that can help guide you now.

ONE

THE BEST OF LIFE

The Good Times Sour

Man, being reasonable, must get drunk;
The best of life is but intoxication:

Lord Byron, *Don Juan*

Everywhere you go; everywhere you look. The focus of every meal and celebration. A bar on each corner. Medicine cabinets crammed with drugs. You never realize how pervasive intoxicants are until you try to stop. The cruise line advertisement shows a tiny ship sailing across the surface of a martini—as if drink were the voyage, the destination, the ocean itself. As if you can't drink at home.

Eventually you might realize that it isn't the world so much as you. That you have become one of those who, as Thoreau wrote, "mistake their private ail for an infected atmosphere." Your mind has slipped into this rut and is mired in obsession. Now you have to find a way out.

When first facing recovery, you want desperately to run back to your old world—so familiar and comforting, the path ahead steep and uncertain. To reassure yourself that it's still there. You're still you. That strange new life, featuring some strange new you, can start tomorrow.

And while that's a bad idea—you'll only end up, a day or a week or a year later, right back where you are now, or worse—it's helpful to pause and look at it for a moment, realize that it was both great and not at all great. Is this the most important thing in your life? It's become that, true, but is this really how you want your story to end? A vital skill in recovery is the ability to think about the what-comes-next part, "consequences," as we tell children. Look at it all. Not just the joy of the first drink but the jolt of the tenth—the hangover after the party, your shame, the hopes of everybody you love dashed.

Even Byron, that romantic idol, fond of wine, debauchery, and revolution, followed his lines about the necessity of drunkenness with the inevitable result. The poem continues:

But to return—get very drunk; and when
    You wake with head-ache, you shall see what then.

Ring for your valet—bid him quickly bring
    Some hock and soda-water . . .

Hock is German white wine. Hock and soda water being the early nineteenth-century version of a wine spritzer. Not the most romantic beverage; then again, the glittering image always has something spattered on it if you look closely. Byron sees clearly enough to capture the whole cycle in a dozen lines: the joy of life shifts to the joy of repairing the damage. Indulgence moves seamlessly from an opportunity to an anticipation to an obligation. At first you use it to feel wonderful, then you use it to feel normal. First you want to, then you have to. You don't even realize what is happening—take comfort in that, in the understanding that this problem is, at least in this sense, not your fault. Nobody wants to become an alcoholic. "You don't decide to be an addict," William S. Burroughs writes in *Junky*. "One morning you wake up sick and you're an addict." It happens when the pleasure you clutch at clutches you and won't let go. Which is one way of thinking about the recovery process: not so much about *you* letting go of something—were it that easy—but about finding a way to make something let go of you. Because the two are intertwined, and while you were grabbing at your substance, your substance was grabbing you.

    "It was not always with me," begins Rainer Maria Rilke's "Song of the Drunkard." "It would come and go."

I wanted to hold it. The wine held it for me.
What it was, I no longer know.
But I was the one being held, held this way and that,

until I could do nothing else.
I, fool.

Now I am trapped in his game. . . .

Many are trapped. Are they fools? They are ordinarily intelli-
gent people who in this regard don't know any better, who insist
they choose to live in bondage. They are not ready. They can't do it,
or, rather, believe they can't. But you are ready. You can do something else. At least you hope you can, or suspect you can, which
is enough. You already *are* doing something just by reading this.
Don't torture yourself with regret about giving up your addiction
forever. You are trying something new, for a day, a week, a year.
How many years have you already spent in your old life? Why not
try something different and go to a new place? Just for a while.
Maybe you will like it there. Take one step, even if it seems impossible, by looking at what you had, what you loved, what it became,
and then say goodbye to it, for now or forever.

•

All ways led to the saloon.

Jack London, *John Barleycorn*

•

At a tavern, there is a general freedom from anxiety. You are sure you are welcome: and the more noise you make, the more trouble you give, the more good things you call for, the welcomer you are . . . there is nothing which has yet been contrived by man, by which so much happiness is produced as by a good tavern or inn.

Samuel Johnson, quoted in *The Life of Samuel Johnson*

•

Bring in the bottled lightning, a clean tumbler, and a corkscrew.

Charles Dickens, *The Life and Adventures of Nicholas Nickleby*

•

A martini makes an ordinary glass shine like a diamond at a coronation, makes an iron bed in Mexico seem like the feather bed of a sultan, a hotel room like the terminus and climax of all voyages, the pinnacle of contentment, the place of repose in an altitude hungered for by all the restless ones.

Anaïs Nin, diary entry, summer 1953

•

What beauty can compare to that of a cantina in the early morning?

Malcolm Lowry, *Under the Volcano*

•

all the best of life . . .
then daydreaming to drink at six,
waiting for the iced fire,
even the feel of the frosted glass,
like waiting for a girl . . .
if you had waited.

Robert Lowell, "For John Berryman"

•

On a busy night familiar greetings would ring out from old friends when de Kooning entered the bar. "Hiya, fellas," de Kooning would say. "Hiya, fellas." . . . From the crowd, Elaine, smoking and chatting, would toss him a wave. Rauschenberg would smile. Frank O'Hara and Mercedes Matter would make room for him at the bar.

Mark Stevens and Annalyn Swan, *de Kooning*

•

In places where drinks are served, you drink. As soon as my glass is empty, the waiter comes over to inquire; if I don't empty it fast enough, he prowls around me, looking at me reproachfully.

Simone de Beauvoir, diary entry, January 28, 1947

1

•

Most of those at the Algonquin roundtable drank their lunch. I thought of drinking the way I now think of gas you put in the car. You get to a place where it is available, you pour it into the opening intended for it, and your car will go for miles until it needs more. I thought of gas not as a diminishing commodity, not as the oil companies' exclusive hold on our economy, or the environment's flirtation with destruction. I thought of it as the substance that makes the automobile move: so I thought scotch and soda, its beautiful amber color, its place in a glass sliding down the bar toward some eager hand, was just the normal way of things, the lubricant of art, its mundane grain-brewed muse.

Anne Roiphe, *Art and Madness*

•

RICHARD:
Give me a bowl of wine.
I have not that alacrity of spirit
Nor cheer of mind that I was wont to have.
Set it down.

William Shakespeare, *Richard III*

•

. . . if the storm within gets too loud, I take a glass too much to stun myself.

Vincent van Gogh, letter to his brother Theo, July 22, 1888

•

Only a drink makes me feel alive at all.

Eugene O'Neill, letter to his wife, February 1920

•

I can't seem to get used to myself. I don't even know if I *am* me. Then as soon as I take a drink, the lead slips away and I recognize myself, I become me again.

Eugene Ionesco, *Rhinoceros*

•

Now he was feeling just swell. *This* was the way to be. Relaxed and calm and warm inside, warm toward all the world. Thoroughly at home and at ease in yourself. What a boon liquor could be when you used it right. He was being the very soul of propriety; temperate, controlled, very gentlemanlike in fact. The drinks were hardly affecting him at all. He could even speed things up a little. Might as well get *some* lift out of the afternoon, specially when you'd had such a slow start. He told Sam to pour him another.

Charles Jackson, *The Lost Weekend*

•

You can show me no man who knows how he began to crave that which he craves. He has not been led to that pass by forethought; he has been driven to it by impulse. Fortune attacks us as often as we attack Fortune. It is dis-

1

graceful, instead of proceeding ahead, to be carried along, and then suddenly, amid the whirlpool of events, to ask in a dazed way: "How did I get into this condition?"

Seneca, Epistle 37

•

Voluntarily or involuntarily, of choice or of necessity, most moderns lead a nerve-racking life, and are continually too tired to be capable of enjoyment without the help of alcohol.

Bertrand Russell, *The Conquest of Happiness*

•

Well, my self-consciousness was such that I simply had to take that drink. So I took it, and another one, and then, lo, the miracle! That strange barrier that had existed between me and all men and women seemed to instantly go down. I felt that I belonged where I was, belonged to life; I belonged to the universe; I was a part of things at last. Oh, the magic of those first three or four drinks! I became the life of the party. I actually could please the guests; I could talk freely, volubly; I could talk well.

Bill Wilson, *Bill W. and Mr. Wilson*

•

Shooting was thrilling. As the experienced cats explained, shooting is more efficient than snorting. Because it goes straight to your bloodstream, you need less to get high.

And then there's the cotton, the sifter, the spoon, the cooking, the needle, the penetration. The self-infliction. The ritual.

Etta James, *Rage to Survive*

•

We have faith in poison.
We will give our lives completely, every day.

Arthur Rimbaud, "Drunken Morning"

•

So I go and get another beer. The supply is already running out. I only had five cans. It is a hot night. Where will I be when the dark falls and the dragons come and there is no more beer?

Thomas Merton, journal entry, June 23, 1966

•

Though I never took a drink before or during the show, I was prone to excesses. What I would do is drink after a performance. A couple of drinks in the dressing room and then I'd go out and have a couple more and then go home. I never thought it would catch up to me. I thought it was social drinking: "Oh, I had two or three drinks." Three drinks were actually nine drinks. I made all kinds of excuses. "So I drink, so what? What's a couple of drinks?" Before I knew it, it was a bottle a night.

Sid Caesar, *Caesar's Hours*

1

•

I found the tide of wine and wassail fast gaining on the dry land of sober judgment.

Washington Irving, *The Keeping of Christmas at Bracebridge Hall*

•

I leave my typewriter at quarter after ten and wander down stairs to the pantry where the bottles are. I do not touch the bottles. I do not even look at the bottles and I congratulate myself fatuously on my will-power. At eleven I make another trip to the pantry and congratulate myself once more but at twelve when the bull-horn blows I fly down the stairs and pour out a scoop. The same thing happens in the afternoon. I take long walks, split wood, paint trim and shovel snow and while I exclaim loudly over the beauty of the winter light there lurks at the back of my mind the image of a bottle of sour-mash. It seems to be, most of the time, an equal struggle.

John Cheever, letter to Josephine Herbst, May 1968

•

When I got back to Los Angeles I found a cheap hotel just off Hoover Street and stayed in bed and drank. I drank for some time, three or four days. I couldn't get myself to read the want ads. The thought of sitting in front of a man behind a desk and telling him that I wanted a job, that I was qualified for a job, was too much for me. Frankly, I was horrified by life, at what a man had to do simply in order to eat, sleep, and keep himself clothed. So I stayed in bed and drank. When you drank the world was still out there, but for the moment it didn't have you by the throat.

Charles Bukowski, *Factotum*

•

Lately I've been
running by day,
drinking by night,
as though first to build
a man and then destroy
him — this for
three months, and
I don't find it foolish
— a man almost 50
who still knows so
little of why he's
alive and would turn
away from answers,
turn to the blankness
that follows my nights
or the pounding of
the breath, the sweat
oiling every part
of me, running
even from my hair.

Philip Levine, "Words"

•

How on earth do I know what I'm going to do, except that it's fairly plain that I will go on drinking and drinking and drinking, and having a good time in bed whenever I can and hitting the keys of my new "Olympia" typewriter — a good one — Ah, well. Goodnight.

Tennessee Williams, *Notebooks*, April 1, 1957

•

It's not the folly of foolishness that's shameful;
The shame is not knowing when folly's time is over.

Horace, "To the Manager of His Farm"

TWO

I DON'T WANT TO DO THAT

The End of the Party

I'll just stop in, he thought, and see if there are any messages; I'll see if there have been any phone calls. He hadn't been back to the hotel, after all, for—let's see—for almost five hours; just wandering around. There might be some messages. I'll just stop in, he thought, and see; and maybe I'll have one brandy. I don't want to sit there in the lobby again and drink brandy; I don't want to do that.

James Thurber, "One Is a Wanderer"

James Thurber is remembered for his classic tale of timid male fantasy, "The Secret Life of Walter Mitty," as well as for his fond recollections of early twentieth-century Columbus, Ohio, and his looping, distinctive cartoons that Dorothy Parker compared to un-baked cookies.

But all wasn't nostalgia and beloved dogs. Occasionally he'd write a bleak, not-at-all-funny story such as "One Is a Wanderer," about a man walking around New York City on a slushy February day, lonely and killing time. He ends up—as he always does—back in the lobby of his hotel, drinking brandy. "I think maybe I'll call the Bradleys," he muses, standing up, realizing only then how much he's drunk: "And don't, he said to himself, standing still a moment, don't tell me you're not cockeyed now, because you are cockeyed now, just as you said you wouldn't be when you got up this morn-ing and had orange juice and coffee and determined to get some work done, a whole lot of work done; just as you said you wouldn't be but you knew you would be, all right."

That is the core, the famous denial that lies at the heart of ad-diction. You realize there is a problem and you pretend you don't.

"That's the way alcoholism works," Caroline Knapp writes in *Drinking*. "You know and you don't know. Or, more accurately, you know and the part of you that wants no part of this knowledge immediately slips into gear, sliding the fear into a new category. You wake up in the morning and—presto!—it's reclassified: *a little problem with drinking*, something you'll take care of when you're less depressed."

You wander as if you didn't know where you're going to end up, as if it were random and a surprise. Drug addicts go to see friends who happen to be dealers. Drunks go to plays and dinners, parties and weddings, doing their best to overlook that the pressing question—where's the bar?—is the same wherever they go.

Some never get beyond denial. Jack London knew he had a drinking problem—he wrote a memoir about it, *John Barleycorn*, frankly detailing an adult life that eventually bordered on near-continual inebriation: "I achieved a condition in which my body was never free from alcohol. Nor did I permit myself to be away from alcohol. If I traveled to out-of-the-way places, I declined to run the risk of finding them dry. I took a quart, or several quarts, along in my grip. In the past I had been amazed by other men guilty of this practice. Now I did it myself unblushingly. . . . There was no time, in all my waking time, that I didn't want a drink."

After an entire book of this, cataloging a thirst that saw him taking his first cocktail of the day before noon, London comes to a startling conclusion, based on his ability to go without drinking during one leg of an ocean voyage: "This I take to show how intrinsically I am not an alcoholic. . . . Thus, once again I proved to my complete satisfaction that I was John Barleycorn's master. I could drink when I wanted, refrain when I wanted. Therefore I would continue to drink when I wanted."

London ends *John Barleycorn* by announcing, "I decided; I shall take my drink on occasion . . . decided coolly and deliberately that I should continue to do what I had been trained to want to do. I would drink—but, oh, more skillfully, more discreetly, than ever before." Three years later he was dead, at age forty.

This sort of fierce denial is common, and so a jarring incident, or, more likely, a series of escalating incidents, is usually required before change is contemplated. Those confronting their addiction begin by addressing the crisis and, only then, are forced to understand the routine that led to it. The beginning of a new life is the gradual realization—the honesty emphasized in AA—that there is a sameness to addiction, a dreariness, a drudgery. It is the identical thing happening over and over again, every day, with only one avenue of escape, one possibility of change, an option that, viewed by a person sunk in the routine of dependence, at first seems incredible, unimaginable, ridiculous. That first step—whether taken on your own or pushed to it by somebody else—is recognizing that you aren't doing this of your own will. It's a compulsion. You don't think using your substance is fun because it's fun to be constantly scourged with the need for drink or drugs. You think it's fun because it's what you do all the time and you're secretly terrified at the thought of not doing it, of enduring the awful hunger you suffer when you stop even briefly. It's like a bad job that you keep telling yourself you must like, because you go there every day and it's all you've got. Addiction is not a bad choice. It's an obsession: grinding, dictatorial, relentless. The great thing about sobriety is that you don't have to succumb to your addiction every day. You don't have to spend your life doing this.

•

Drugs are a carnival in hell. There're merry-go-rounds and roller coasters. You shoot up, you rocket down; you go up again, you come down again.... Everything's like everything else, always the same; monotonous; gray; dirty. But you don't even notice, you go right on....

Edith Piaf, *Piaf*

•

There was nothing to do but to drink . . . each day became a replica of the day before.

Ernest Hemingway, unpublished draft of *The Sun Also Rises*

•

God, how pointless and empty the world is! Days filled with cheap and tarnished moments succeed each other, restless and haunted nights follow in bitter routine: the sun shines without brightness, and the moon rises without light.

Malcolm Lowry, *Under the Volcano*

•

I had a straight shot
from the bottle, then
a drink of warm collins mix,
then another whisky.
And though I went from room
to room, no one was home.
What luck, I thought.

> Years later,
> I still wanted to give up
> friends, love, starry skies,
> for a house where no one
> was home, no one coming back,
> and all I could drink.

Raymond Carver, "Luck"

·

> More, more, I think—all of it, to the last exquisite drop, for there is no satiety for me, nor ever has been, in such drinking.

M. F. K. Fisher, "G Is for Gluttony"

·

> But the same stimulus to the human organism will not continue to produce the same response. By and by I discovered there was no kick at all in one cocktail. One cocktail left me dead. There was no glow, no laughter tickle. Two or three cocktails were required to produce the original effect of one. And I wanted that effect. I drank my first cocktail at eleven-thirty when I took the morning's mail into the hammock....

Jack London, *John Barleycorn*

·

As for quenching his thirst, liquor did exactly the opposite. To quench is to slake or to satisfy, to give you enough. Liquor couldn't do that. One drink led inevitably to the next, more demanded more, they became progressively easier and easier, culminating in the desperate need, no longer easy, that shook him on days such as these. His need to breathe was not more urgent.

Charles Jackson, *The Lost Weekend*

•

Vices are never genuinely tamed. Again, if reason prevails, the passions will not even get a start; but if they get under way against the will of reason, they will maintain themselves against the will of reason. For it is easier to stop them in the beginning than to control them when they gather force. This half-way ground is accordingly misleading and useless; it is to be regarded just as the declaration that we ought to be "moderately" insane, or "moderately" ill. Virtue alone possesses moderation; the evils that afflict the mind do not admit of moderation. You can more easily remove than control them.

Seneca, Epistle 85

•

After two drinks, a close friend said, de Kooning became a brilliant raconteur and conversationalist. Before that he was too reserved; later, too drunk.

Mark Stevens and Annalyn Swan, *de Kooning*

•

He and Al Shockley had been alcoholics. They had sought each other out like two castoffs who were still social enough to prefer drowning together to doing it alone. The sea had been whole grain instead of salt, that was all. . . . He was *still* an alcoholic, always would be, perhaps had been since Sophomore Class Night in high school when he had taken his first drink. It had nothing to do with willpower, or the morality of drinking, or the weakness or strength of his own character. There was a broken switch somewhere inside, or a circuit breaker that didn't work, and he had been propelled down the chute willy-nilly, slowly at first, then accelerating.... All his life he had been trying unsuccessfully to control it.

Stephen King, *The Shining*

.

He began to grow disgusted with himself for waiting so anxiously for the promised arrival of something that had stopped being fun anyway. He didn't even know why he liked it anymore. It made his mouth dry and his eyes dry and red and his face sag, and he hated it when his face sagged, it was as if all the integrity of all the muscles in his face was eroded by marijuana, and he got terribly self-conscious about the fact that his face was sagging, and had long ago forbidden himself to smoke dope around anyone else. He didn't even know what its draw was anymore.

David Foster Wallace, *Infinite Jest*

.

2

What time is it? Heroin. What are you doing tomorrow? Heroin. Why are you going to the hospital? Heroin. What are your plans when you get out? Heroin. Written anything lately? Heroin.

Seth Mnookin, "Harvard and Heroin"

•

I don't want you to think I'm a drinker. I can stop any time I want to — only I don't want to.

Billy Wilder and I. A. L. Diamond, *Some Like It Hot*

•

Booze will send me to never-never land, dress me in thick wool, earmuff me against the voices, blink off the light, give rest and sleep and peace. Just what I must have wanted. Just what I don't want.

Geoffrey Wolff, *A Day at the Beach*

•

You cannot selectively numb emotion. You can't say: here's the bad stuff. Here's vulnerability, here's grief, here's shame, here's fear, here's disappointment. I don't want to feel these. I'm going to have a couple of beers and a banana nut muffin. I don't want to feel these. . . . You can't numb those hard feelings without numbing the other affects, our emotions. You cannot selectively numb. So when you numb those, we numb joy. We numb gratitude. We numb happiness. And then we are miserable.

Brené Brown, TED talk

•

Life, friends, is boring. We must not say so.
After all, the sky flashes, the great sea yearns,
we ourselves flash and yearn,

and moreover my mother told me as a boy
(repeatingly) "Ever to confess you're bored
means you have no

Inner Resources." I conclude now I have no
inner resources, because I am heavy bored.

John Berryman, "The Dream Songs"

•

I positively dread retirement. I have no "inner resources,"
no interests, nothing to fall back on. Nothing but the pub
and the bottle. And the *Times* crossword. But shall I be able
to afford these? I doubt it.

Philip Larkin, letter to Judy Egerton, June 9, 1983

•

Francis felt healthy and he liked it. It's too bad he didn't
feel healthy when he drank. He felt good then but not
healthy, especially not in the morning, or when he woke
up in the middle of the night, say. Sometimes he felt dead.

William Kennedy, *Ironweed*

•

It was at this time I became aware of waiting with expec-
tancy for the pre-dinner cocktail. I *wanted* it, and I was *con-
scious* that I wanted it.

Jack London, *John Barleycorn*

2

•

In church, on my knees before the chancel, I see, with a crushing force, how dependent I am on alcohol.

John Cheever, journal entry, 1963

•

My Uncle Wight, Mr. Talbott, and others were with us, and we were pretty merry. So at night home and to bed — finding my head grow weak nowadays if I come to drink wine; and therefore hope that I shall leave it off of myself, which I pray God I could do.

Samuel Pepys, diary entry, May 14, 1661

•

And the commencement of atonement is
The sense of its necessity.

Lord Byron, *Manfred*

•

I realized that I could never go out of the house again without liquor. Orange juice and bourbon in the morning was not enough. The physical demand was growing. I would need liquor more often — not because I wanted it, but because my nerves required it. Since I was a judge's wife, I couldn't be seen dropping into bars: I must carry my own liquor. That day I bought small two-ounce medicine bottles in the drug store, filled them with liquor, and thereafter was never without a couple in my purse.

Soon I was slipping down doorways, vanishing into ladies' rooms, anywhere I could gain privacy, to take a swift drink to ward off the spells that came upon me with increasing frequency. The two-ounce bottles graduated to six-ounce, and then to a pint, and in the last years of my marriage to the judge, wherever I went, I carried a fifth of liquor in my bag.

Lillian Roth, *I'll Cry Tomorrow*

•

. . . it is difficult to get enough of something that doesn't quite work.

Dr. Vincent Felitti, "The Origins of Addiction"

•

Men sink themselves in pleasures, and they cannot do without them when once they have become accustomed to them, and for this reason they are most wretched, because they have reached such a pass that what was once superfluous to them has become indispensable. And so they are the slaves of their pleasures instead of enjoying them; they even love their own ills—and that is the worst ill of all! Then it is that the height of unhappiness is reached, when men are not only attracted, but even pleased, by shameful things, and when there is no longer any room for a cure, now that those things which once were vices have become habits.

Seneca, Epistle 39

2

•

For in so far as drinking is really a sin it is not because drinking is wild, but because drinking is tame; not in so far as it is anarchy, but in so far as it is slavery. Probably the worst way to drink is to drink medicinally. Certainly the safest way to drink is to drink carelessly; that is, without caring much for anything, and especially not caring for the drink.

G. K. Chesterton, *All Things Considered*

•

I see the better way and approve it, but I follow the worse way.

Ovid, *Metamorphoses*

•

I await with patience a catastrophe that is slow in coming.

Albert Camus, notebook entry, December 1951

•

"How did you go bankrupt?" Bill asked.
"Two ways," Mike said. "Gradually and then suddenly."

Ernest Hemingway, *The Sun Also Rises*

•

Drinking heavily, you abandon people — and they abandon you — and you abandon yourself.

Jack Kerouac, *Some of the Dharma*

•

Addiction is lonely. It starts as pure pleasure, and the degeneration, in a few quick years, into a form of monumental compulsive-obsessive condition is actually more psychological than physical. Once the drug use has replaced everything else, life becomes purely a lie, since in order to keep any self-respect, the junkie has to delude himself that use is by choice. That's the worst loneliness — the isolation, even from oneself, in that lie. In the meantime the original physical pleasure becomes merely dull relief from the threat of withdrawal, from the horror of real life.

Richard Hell, *I Dreamed I Was a Very Clean Tramp*

•

I shot into the back of my hands. I didn't start the day without pumping some coke into a vein somewhere. Thanks again to Dr. D, I had learned how to inject myself. If I was alone, I'd get some rubber tubing, slip it in a knot around my arm, yank a loose end in my teeth with a jerk of the head to raise a vein, then shoot. We were spending less and less time out and around town because we needed to keep shooting. The craving was a desperate, blinding compulsion. I would sometimes have to shoot up every fifteen minutes.

John Phillips, *Papa John*

2

•

I wish you knew me before I was like this.

Gil Scott-Heron, quoted in the *New Yorker*

•

After three quick double whiskies I felt better: I was drunk, in fact, drunk with that pristine freshness, that semi-mystical elevation of spirit which, every time, seems destined to last for ever.

Kingsley Amis, *The Green Man*

•

It is often tragic to see how blatantly a man bungles his own life and the lives of others yet remains totally incapable of seeing how much the whole tragedy originates in himself, and how he continually feeds it and keeps it going. Not *consciously*, of course — for consciously he is engaged in bewailing and cursing a faithless world that recedes further and further into the distance. Rather, it is an unconscious factor which spins the illusions that veil his world. And what is being spun is a cocoon, which in the end will completely envelop him.

C. G. Jung, *Aion*

•

At the end of my drinking, the kingdom I longed for, slaved for, and at the end of each day lunged at was a rickety slab of unreal estate about four foot square — a back stair landing off my colonial outside Cambridge, Mass. I'd sit hunched against the door guzzling whiskey and smoking Marlboros while wires from a tinny Walkman piped blues into my head. Though hours there were frequently spent howling inwardly about the melting ice floe of my marriage, this spate of hours was the highlight of my day.

Mary Karr, *Lit*

•

 Desperation is the raw material of drastic change. Only those who can leave behind everything they have ever believed in can hope to escape.

William S. Burroughs, *The Western Lands*

•

I wonder if I am becoming allergic to alcohol. These days drink all too frequently produces in me a terrible mixture of fatigue and illness, as if I were going to die. My belly is enormous. My spirits droop like a flag of truce. My attempts to "cut down" are puny, like having five drinks instead of six, and have not the slightest effect of any kind. This ill-feeling may be Nature's aversion therapy. I will keep you posted.

Philip Larkin, letter to Anthony Thwaite, November 4, 1984

•

It was one of those midsummer Sundays when everyone sits around saying, "I *drank* too much last night."

John Cheever, "The Swimmer"

•

2

A small note after a large orgy. It is morning, gray, most sober, with cold white puritanical eyes; looking at me. Last night I got drunk, very very beautifully drunk, and now I am shot, after six hours of warm sleep like a baby, with Racine to read, and not even the energy to type; I am getting the dts. Or something.

Sylvia Plath, journal entry, February 26, 1956

•

Snuggling luxuriously on a pillow, I said, "There won't be a next time."

Emily Hahn, *The Big Smoke*

•

What had happened? She still wondered and still had not the slightest idea. The subject was taboo between them. He was like a man who had leaned around a corner and had seen an unexpected monster lying in wait, crouching among the dried bones of its old kills. The liquor remained in the cabinet, but he didn't touch it. She had considered throwing them out a dozen times but in the end always backed away from the idea, as if some unknown charm would be broken by the act.

Stephen King, *The Shining*

•

One day, gorgeous as usual, I'm walking to the store and two short sentences pass through my head: I'm an alcoholic. I need help. I have no idea where these thoughts come from, nor do I really understand what they mean, but I know that they're true.

Domenica Ruta, *With or Without You*

•

The eyes that fix you in a formulated phrase,
And when I am formulated, sprawling on a pin,
When I am pinned and wriggling on the wall,
Then how should I begin
To spit out all the butt-ends of my days and ways?

T. S. Eliot, "The Love Song of J. Alfred Prufrock"

•

The delusion under which I was operating then was that alcohol would open me up and make me more insightful as to human psychology, but just the opposite turned out to be the case. It ended up being a real hindrance as far as writing goes. It blunted me, it made me self-centered, anxious, avoidant, unable to understand or identify the motives of others. And I think that's been true of other writers, too — Exley, Fitzgerald, Faulkner, Yeats, Hemingway, Burroughs, Kerouac. There are many, many examples. You can see alcohol beginning to endanger what was valuable about the work of these writers, until, ultimately, the work reflects only its abuse.

Rick Moody, interview, *The Paris Review*

•

2

Thinking again, in the dentist's chair, that I am like a prisoner who is trying to escape from jail by the wrong route. For all one knows, that door may stand open, although I continue to dig a tunnel with a teaspoon.

John Cheever, journal entry, 1952

•

That night, in a shabby little dressing room off the kitchen of the Hotel Regina, I made a life decision. I walked off the stage into the dressing room, sat down, and looked at myself in the mirror. I took a real good look. I asked myself, "Sid, do you want to live or do you want to die?" It was simple as that. There was no gray area, no maybe, no if, no nothing. "That's it," I said. "I can't. No more." I decided that I was going to live.

Sid Caesar, *Caesar's Hours*

•

I have a theory that every time you make an important choice, the part of you left behind continues the other life you could have had.

Jeanette Winterson, *Oranges Are Not the Only Fruit*

•

That Which I Should Have Done I Did Not Do

Ivan Albright, painting title

•

His gaze, forever blocked by bars,
is so exhausted it takes in nothing else.
All that exists for him are a thousand bars.
Beyond the thousand bars, no world.

The strong, supple pacing
moves in narrowing circles.
It is a dance at whose center
a great will is imprisoned.

Now and again the veil over his pupils
silently lifts. An image enters,
pierces the numbness,
and dies away in his heart.

> **Rainer Maria Rilke,** "The Panther"

•

The crack is moving down the wall.
Defective plaster isn't all the cause.
We must remain until the roof falls in.

It's mildly cheering to recall
That every building has its little flaws.
The crack is moving down the wall.

Here in the kitchen, drinking gin,
We can accept the damndest laws.
We must remain until the roof falls in.

> **Weldon Kees,** "Five Villanelles"

2

•

Houses crack before they crash.

> **Seneca,** Epistle 103

•

Because we lived our several lives
Caught up within the spells of love.
Because we always had to run
Through the enormous yards of day
To do all that we hoped to do,
We did not hear, beneath our lives,
The old walls falling out of true,
Foundations shifting in the dark.
When seedlings blossomed in the eaves,
When branches scratched upon the door
And rain came splashing through the halls,
We made our minor, brief repairs,
And sang upon the crumbling stairs
And danced upon the sodden floors.
For years we lived at peace, until
The rooms themselves began to blend
With time, and empty one by one,
At which we knew, with muted hearts,
That nothing further could be done,
And so rose up, and went away,
Inheritors of breath and love,
Bound to that final black estate
No child can mend or trade away.

Mary Oliver, "The House"

•

When he was in his last clinic some friends came in a group to tell him that they could no longer bear witness to his self-destruction, if he didn't stop drinking, at least for a while, they would close their doors to him. He replied that he was sorry, but he couldn't contemplate life without alcohol. There was a long silence, and then one of them said, "Well, Piers, you've just announced the end of our friendship." And they left. A few weeks later he collapsed with a burst liver, burst kidneys, burst everything, really. His death caught him by surprise, I think—I certainly don't think he intended it, even though he did it by his own hand—but perhaps he had no choice, who knows? He certainly behaved as if he thought he hadn't, and all in all I'm pretty sure he wanted to go on living, if only to go on drinking.

Simon Gray, *The Smoking Diaries*

•

Footfalls echo in the memory
Down the passage which we did not take
Towards the door we never opened
Into the rose-garden.

T. S. Eliot, "Burnt Norton"

•

Disaster can be a fine designer. Better than pencil sometimes. It can lead you to safety.

David Esterly, *The Lost Carving*

2

•

When the beginnings of self-destruction enter the heart it seems no bigger than a grain of sand. It is a headache, a slight case of indigestion, an infected finger; but you miss the 8:20 and arrive late at the meeting on credit extensions. The old friend that you meet for lunch suddenly exhausts your patience and in an effort to be pleasant you drink three cocktails, but by now the day has lost its form, its sense and meaning. To try and restore some purpose and beauty to it you drink too much at cocktails you talk too much you make a pass at somebody's wife and you end with doing something foolish and obscene and wish in the morning that you were dead. But when you try to trace back the way you came into this abyss all you find is a grain of sand.

John Cheever, journal entry, 1952

·

It is the speck that makes the cloud that wrecks the vessel, children, yet no one fears a speck.

Emily Dickinson, letter to Louise and
Frances Norcross, October 1871

·

One doesn't discover new lands without consenting to lose sight of the shore for a very long time.

André Gide, *The Counterfeiters*

·

You may do this, I tell you, it is permitted.
Begin again the story of your life.

Jane Hirshfield, "Da Capo"

THREE

THE DIRECTION YOU LEAST TRUST

Making the Leap

When you are completely off balance, so much so that you are certain you will topple over—you bring the paddle down hard on the water's surface, the way ducks bat their wings. You will feel your kayak right itself. Only by moving in the direction you least trust can you be saved.

Roger Rosenblatt, *Kayak Morning*

If you've ever flipped a kayak, you know how unsettling it can be to suddenly find yourself underwater, upside down, careening along a river of unknown bottom landscape. Not a time for deliberation. Instead, instinct and experience must kick in, to get back upright on the breezy side of the water's surface. There will be time later to indulge in speculation about what went wrong.

When most people think of recovery, they think of the very beginning. The celebrity disappears into "rehab," whatever that is. Some public humiliation causes a heretofore respected individual to announce that he or she is going to seek help with "demons," with a drinking problem, or a hazy issue involving medication. Specifics are often hard to come by. The veil is drawn and the decent thing to do is look away, let the troubled person alone, and grant that individual the necessary space to get better.

When that troubled person is you, however, there is no polite turning away, no veil, no escape. "No matter where you go," in the immortal words of Buckaroo Banzai, "there you are." The support you usually depend on—the indulgent spouse, the laughing buddies—aren't so indulgent or good-humored anymore. The former solution to all your problems is suddenly your biggest problem. Not only has your reality soured, but the comfort you relied on even when things were going well has been rudely stripped away, ironically, just when you need it most—when some crisis or embarrassment or tragedy has turned you upside down and forced you into this unwelcome situation. You feel lousy and there is no relief and no prospect of relief. Fate has grabbed you by the seat of the pants and heaved you through the door of recovery, or—in rare cases—you have managed to crawl there yourself, the one direction you don't want to go.

It is an alien, submerged world. Instead of the usual comfort, you find books to read, films to watch, meetings to attend. You reach for solace and grab thorns. Rehab is like going to traffic school for weeks at a time. Your old friends are achingly absent; enter your new friends, emissaries from the dry world of sobriety. Strangers in plaid flannel who want to hug you while you draw back. You narrow your eyes at the cheerless cinder-block church basement where your support group meets, rate the inadequacy of the coffee, the banal specifics of the other people in your meeting: the overly inquisitive buzz-cut guy, for instance, who welcomes you too cheerily. This, he insists, is a happy development, something you should have been looking forward to. He tells you that quitting is the best thing that will ever happen to you, that getting sober—twenty-nine years and counting!—is the best thing that ever happened to him. Or the meeting bully ready to leap on what he considers your mistaken notions, as if you're supposed to walk in the door with this stuff down cold. The disheveled woman in a hat that looks like a shower cap who rambles on. These are your peers now.

That may be what you think, but . . . brace yourself . . . it doesn't matter what you think. Your thinking is what has gotten you into this mess. At this point you must somehow suspend your critical scrutiny. As hard as it may be to accept, for the time being your opinions don't count. You've done your thinking and made your decisions, based on an awareness that has become twisted by addiction—some part of you must know that. You wouldn't have done the things you've done if your judgment weren't skewed. Now is not the time to minimize, to rationalize, to deny. Now is the time for truth, for soul searching, and for surrender. This is a difficult process; at times rehab is like attending the autopsy of someone you love. Try to focus on the courage required for honesty and not necessarily on the specifics of what you are being honest about. "How beautiful is candor!" Walt Whitman writes in *Leaves of Grass*. "All faults may be forgiven of him who has perfect candor."

You're here to learn something new, not cling to something old. Put your trust in others. Suppress your ego, listen to these unfamiliar people, including the disheveled woman in the awful hat. She is further along than you. She may have something to teach you. You're underwater—you have to right yourself.

The bad news is, this is the hardest part, the part that some people must go through again and again. The good news is, this is the hardest part, and every hour, every day, every week the process will get easier, more or less, if you stay the course and tack toward this new life that you don't want and can't yet imagine, a life that will someday seem so much more valuable and hard-won than the life that came before.

•

Rowing with just one oar
I lost that oar

For the first time I looked round at the wide stretch of water

Ko Un, "Flowers of a Moment"

•

Ripeness is all. Come on.

Shakespeare, *King Lear*

•

Sorrow is an angel
that comes to you in blue light
and shows you what is wrong
just to see if you'll set it right
and I've fucked up so many times
in my life —
that I want to get it right this time.

Frank Orrall, "Complicated"

•

I have newly taken a solemn oath about abstaining from
plays and wine, which I am resolved to keep according to
the letter of the oath which I keep by me.

Samuel Pepys, diary entry, December 31, 1661

•

These passions, which are heavy taskmasters, sometimes ruling by turns, and sometimes together, can be banished from you by wisdom, which is the only real freedom. There is but one path leading thither, and it is a straight path; you will not go astray. Proceed with steady step, and if you would have all things under your control, put yourself under the control of reason.

Seneca, Epistle 37

•

✳It's never the changes we want that change everything.

Junot Díaz, *The Brief Wondrous Life of Oscar Wao*

•

This storm irresistibly propels him into the future to which his back is turned, while the pile of debris before him grows skyward. This storm is what we call progress.

Walter Benjamin, *Theses on the Philosophy of History*

3

•

Well I'm gone to Detox Mansion
Way down on Last Breath Farm

Warren Zevon and Jorge Calderón, "Detox Mansion"

•

Awake ye drunkards, and weepe, and howle all yee drinkers of wine, because of the new wine, for it is cut off from
your mouth.

> **The Book of Joel 1:5,** King James Version

•

Wine I never thought anybody could take away from you.
But they can.

> **Ernest Hemingway,** letter to Archibald MacLeish,
> June 28, 1957

•

My eyes are wide open
Can't get to sleep
One thing I'm sure of
I'm in at the deep freeze
Cold turkey has got me on the run . . .

Thirty-six hours
Rolling in pain
Praying to someone
Free me again

Oh I'll be a good boy
Please make me well
I promise you anything
Get me out of this hell

> **John Lennon,** "Cold Turkey"

•

Why, this is hell, nor am I out of it:
Think'st thou that I, who saw the face of God,
And tasted the eternal joy of heaven,
Am not tormented with ten thousand hells,
In being depriv'd of everlasting bliss?

Christopher Marlowe, "The Tragical History of Dr. Faustus"

•

Will power is nothing. Morals is nothing. Lord, this is illness.

John Berryman, *Recovery*

•

Comforter, where, where is your comforting?

Gerard Manley Hopkins, "No worst, there is none"

•

O despairer, here is my neck,
By God! you shall not go down! Hang your whole weight
    upon me.
I dilate you with tremendous breath.... I buoy you up;
Every room of the house do I fill with an armed force....
    lovers of me,
bafflers of graves:
Sleep! I and they keep guard all night;
Not doubt, not decease shall dare to lay finger upon you,
I have embraced you, and henceforth possess you to myself,

3

And when you rise in the morning you will find what I tell you is so.

Walt Whitman, *Leaves of Grass*

•

The gates of hell are open night and day;
Smooth the descent, and easy is the way
But to retrace your steps, to climb back to the upper air—
There the struggle, there the labor lies.

Virgil, *The Aeneid*

•

Any fool can get into an ocean
But it takes a Goddess
To get out of one.
What's true of oceans is true, of course,
Of labyrinths and poems...
But when you've tried the blessed water long
Enough to want to start backward
That's when the fun starts...
Any Greek can get you into a labyrinth
But it takes a hero to get out of one

Jack Spicer, "Any fool can get into an ocean . . ."

•

No one's a hero just for taking dope. You might be a hero for getting off it. I loved the shit. But enough was enough. Also, it narrowed one's horizons, and eventually all you know are junkies. I had to move to broader horizons. You only know all this, of course, once you've gotten out of there. That's what that stuff does. It's the most seductive bitch in the world.

Keith Richards, *Life*

•

What was it like to be led?

I trusted no one. My name
was like a stranger's,
read from an envelope.

But nothing was taken from me
that I could have used.
For once, I admit that.

Louise Glück, "Tango"

•

I had not thought of myself as a person who could choose. Freedom was a terrible prospect, exhilarating and terrible.

Claire Messud, *The Last Life*

3

•

"So this purports to be a disease, alcoholism? A disease like a cold? Or like cancer? I have to tell you, I have never heard of anyone being told to pray for relief from cancer. Outside maybe certain very rural parts of the American South, that is. So what is this? You're *ordering* me to pray? Because I allegedly have a disease? I dismantle my life and career and enter nine months of low-income treatment for a *disease*, and I'm prescribed prayer? Does the word *retrograde* signify? Am I in a sociohistorical era I don't know about? What exactly is the story here?"

David Foster Wallace, *Infinite Jest*

•

To give a brief definition: by "disease" we mean a persistent perversion of the judgment, so that things which are mildly desirable are thought to be highly desirable. Or, if you prefer, we may define it thus: to be too zealous in striving for things which are only mildly desirable or not desirable at all, or to value highly things which ought to be valued but slightly or valued not at all.

Seneca, Epistle 75

•

Healing . . . is not a science, but the intuitive art of wooing Nature.

W. H. Auden, "The Art of Healing"

•

Do you not see how necessary a World of Pains and troubles is to school an Intelligence and make it a Soul?

John Keats, letter to George and Georgiana Keats, April 21, 1819

•

Why are you so unwilling to let this experience change you?

Dr. Steven Frisch, conversation

•

⚹ These are the days that must happen to you.

Walt Whitman, "Song of the Open Road"

•

There is a point at which everything becomes simple and there is no longer any question of choice, because all you have staked will be lost if you look back. Life's point of no return.

Dag Hammarskjöld, *Markings*

•

What was lost was lost. There was no retrieving it, however you schemed, no returning to how things were, no going back.

Haruki Murakami, *Hard-Boiled Wonderland and the End of the World*

•

3

"He sank so low that every instrument
for his salvation now fell short
except to make him see souls in perdition."

Dante Alighieri, *Purgatorio,* 30

•

There were about thirty guys in a room, many of whom I knew or recognized. The meeting was simple. One guy started it by reading "How It Works," or the twelve steps to sobriety, from the AA Blue Book, then said his name and described his week since the last meeting, staying within the three-minute time limit, which gave everyone a chance to speak.

"I'm glad to be here," I said when it was my turn...

It went around the room like that until the last person had shared his story. Then all of us stood up and said the Serenity Prayer: "God grant me the serenity to accept the things I cannot change, the courage to change the things I can, and the wisdom to know the difference. Amen."

Since that day those Monday night meetings have become an essential part of my life and I've said the prayer every morning after I brush my teeth while looking at a framed photo of my liver donor, which I have courtesy of the *National Enquirer*. It's proved to be one of the most important prayers I've ever known. As soon as I began meditating on it, it opened up a whole new avenue of living—compassion, strength, conviction, and wonder.

Larry Hagman, *Hello Darlin'*

•

All's misalliance.
Yet why not say what happened?

Robert Lowell, "Epilogue"

•

I have been confined since the 9th but I will be let out tomorrow morning to go to church. Mary will visit me tomorrow afternoon. The indoctrination here is stern, evangelical, protestant and tireless. The cast is around forty former drug addicts and clinical alcoholics. The setting is a mansion from the twenties with rooms from other mansions and or castles. Austrian would be my guess. I share a bedroom and a bath with four other men. 1. is an unsuccessful con man. 2. an unsuccessful German delicatessen owner. 3. an unemployable sailor with a troll's face and faded tattoos, and 4. a leading dancer from American Ballet. Our windows look onto the backyards of 92nd street. There are a few dogs, a baritone, a cat, church bells, no voices other than the baritone.

Half the time I know why I'm here; half the time I don't. The conflict is really painful and when it gets me in the middle of the stairs I nearly faint. My release date is the second week in May. I expect you'll be in Maine but I'll see you during the summer. If I stay dry for three months after leaving here I get a free watch-chain but I don't have a pocket watch which is the way my thinking goes.

John Cheever, letter to Arthur Spear, April 19, 1975

3

•

"I cannot help thinking that there is something to admire in every one, even if you do not approve of them."

E. M. Forster, *A Room with a View*

•

Just this, just this, this room where we are. Pay attention to that. Pay attention to who's there, pay attention to what isn't known there, pay attention to what is known there, pay attention to what everyone is thinking and feeling, what you're doing there, pay attention. Pay attention.

W. S. Merwin, *The Buddha*

•

It is now high time to consider what sort of world you are part of, and from what kind of governor of it you are descended; that you have a set period assigned you to act in, and unless you improve it to brighten and compose your thoughts, it will quickly run off with you, and be lost beyond recovery.

Marcus Aurelius, *Meditations*

•

Thirty years ago my older brother, who was ten years old at the time, was trying to get a report on birds written that he'd had three months to write, which was due the next day. We were out at our family cabin in Bolinas, and he was at the kitchen table close to tears, surrounded by binder paper and pencils and unopened books on birds, immobilized by the hugeness of the task ahead. Then my father sat down beside him, put his arm around my brother's shoulder, and said, "Bird by bird, buddy. Just take it bird by bird."

Anne Lamott, *Bird by Bird*

•

Between where you are now and where you'd like to be there's a sort of barrier, or a chasm, and sometimes it's a good idea to imagine that you're already at the other side of that chasm, so that you can start on the unknown side.

David Bohm, quoted by F. David Peat

•

Regret is vain.
Then do not grieve for what you would efface,
The sudden failure of the past, the pain
Of its unwilling change, and the disgrace.

Leave innocence,
And modify your nature by the grief
Which poses to the will indifference
That no desire is permanent in sense.

Take leave of me.
What recompense, or pity, or deceit
Can cure, or what assumed serenity
Conceal the mortal loss which we repeat?

The mind will change, and change shall be relief.

Edgar Bowers, "Amor Vincit Omnia"

•

I began to be sensible of strange feelings. I felt a melting in me. No more my splintered heart and maddened hand were turned against the wolfish world.

Herman Melville, *Moby-Dick*

•

Your heart's in retrograde. You simply have no choice.
Things people told you turn out to be true.
You have to hold that body, hear that voice.
You'd have sworn no one knew you more than you.

How many people thought you'd never change?
But here you have. It's beautiful. It's strange.

Kate Light, "There Comes the Strangest Moment"

•

Hard is trying to rebuild yourself, piece by piece, with no
instruction book, and no clue as to where all the important
bits are supposed to go.

Nick Hornby, *A Long Way Down*

•

It's very hard to stop doing things you're used to doing. You
almost have to dismantle yourself and scatter it all around
and then put a blindfold on and put it back together so that
you avoid old habits.

Tom Waits, quoted in *Lowside of the Road*

•

But then one regrets the loss even of one's worst habits.
Perhaps one regrets them the most. They are such an essential part of one's personality.

Oscar Wilde, *The Picture of Dorian Gray*

•

At night I supped with him at the Mitre Tavern, that we
might renew our social intimacy at the original place of
meeting. But there was now a considerable difference in
his way of living. Having had an illness, in which he was ad-
vised to leave off wine, he had, from that period, continued
to abstain from it, and drank only water, or lemonade.

James Boswell, *The Life of Samuel Johnson*

•

Let me begin again as a speck
of dust caught in the night winds
sweeping out to sea. Let me begin
this time knowing the world is
salt water and dark clouds, the world
is grinding and sighing all night, and dawn
comes slowly and changes nothing. Let
me go back to land after a lifetime
of going nowhere. This time lodged
in the feathers of some scavenging gull
white above the black ship that docks
and broods upon the oily waters of
your harbor...
Tonight I shall enter my life
after being at sea for ages, quietly,
in a hospital named for an automobile.
The one child of millions of children
who has flown alone by the stars
above the black wastes of moonless waters
that stretched forever, who has turned

3

golden in the full sun of a new day.
A tiny wise child who this time will love
his life because it is like no other.

Philip Levine, "Let Me Begin Again"

·

Wave of sorrow,
Do not drown me now:

I see the island
Still ahead somehow.

I see the island
And its sands are fair:

Wave of sorrow,
Take me there.

Langston Hughes, "Island [1]"

FOUR

NOTHING TO LOSE

Early Recovery

Staring moodily down on a half-empty parking lot, he said to himself: "I am at the point of death—physical mental spiritual. Highly promising. I have nothing to lose. There exists the lock, my only concern is the key."

John Berryman, *Recovery*

The crisis ebbs, a little—the initial shock, regret, and confusion of whatever landed you into rehab dials back a few notches. The relentless yearning eases, the hell of detox is over, for the most part. You've gone to your first few meetings. Now you begin the steady trudge forward into this new life of yours.

You might even feel wonderful at times—"the pink cloud," as it's called, a sense of joy at your liberation, at this unfamiliar freedom. So now you're sober. That was easy! A euphoria that, alas, like all euphoria, cannot last. "There is no such thing as a life of passion any more than a continuous earthquake, or an eternal fever," Lord Byron wrote in a letter in 1821. "Besides, who would ever *shave* themselves in such a state?"

Yes, there are people who give it up, walk away, never look back, and are fine. And some people plunge over Niagara Falls and emerge from the maelstrom at the bottom dripping but unharmed. Most, however, are not so lucky. For them there is no easy solution. Alcoholism and addiction are physical compulsions and chronic mental illnesses. Once you cease feeding your obsession, once you stop using the substance you crave, the obsession still remains, the craving dormant, biding its time. Having stopped and feeling great about it does not mean that it won't still come roaring back, unexpectedly, powerfully, corroding your rebuilt life and eroding your determination not to return to old ways.

Unless you find an equally powerful force to replace it.

You can refrain from using the substance that ensnared you, at least for a while. But can you refrain from thinking about it? From regret and sadness and doubt and isolation? Can you build a meaningful life that offers you joy and relaxation without it?

This isn't over yet. The truth is, it will *never* be over, but that's a hard truth and can be set aside for now. You need to brace yourself for the difficult work in front of you. You've got your addiction locked in a cell in the basement. Now you have to see that it stays there.

Just keep in mind that whether you are learning about recovery for an hour at lunch, or every evening, or all day, or locked in a ward for twenty-eight days straight, your time in this setting is limited. Unless you figure out what's happening, once the support stops you will end up right back in the place you're trying to escape—this is a maze that is designed to shunt you back to the starting point. People redo rehab again and again, and if you think it sucks the first time, try the fourth.

If you were about to parachute into the Amazonian jungle, but first were being taught wilderness survival skills, you would pay attention. Rehab is teaching you life survival skills in its own clunky, earnest, and too-direct way with its cheesy videos and hackneyed tracts. Don't be distracted by style. Pay attention to substance. This stuff is important. Before you know it, your parachute will be snapping open above you, the green expanse rushing up from below, and then you'll be on your own.

You can focus on how lousy it is to be here, or you can review your options. John Berryman was a major American poet haunted by the death of his father, who committed suicide when John was twelve. A big, bearded, hard-living man, Berryman realized, "I have nothing to lose," and while he saw rehab as a rude shock from his life of celebrity and celebration, he also knew how important it was that he master his disease. He wrote:

> un-numbing now toward sorting in & out
> I've got to get as little as possible wrong. . . .
>
> I am the king's son who squat down in rags
> declared unfit by wise friends to inherit
> and nothing of me left but skull & feet

Do not look for easy outs. Get as little as possible wrong. Going back to using is an easy out, merely delaying when you have to face this again, making it even harder next time, with fewer loved ones, and one more failure heckling you from the sidelines.

John Berryman eventually killed himself. The impulse is not unusual. Drunks and addicts, faced with a life without their substance, sometimes kill themselves. That's how bleak it can be. Confronted with having to lose one thing in life, they choose instead to lose it all.

There are only two things we know for certain about life and death—the first is that, however long you are alive, you are dead for much, much, much longer. And second, it is a one-way street— there is no returning. Both facts encourage sticking out your time here for as long as possible, painful though it is at the moment. Be stronger than your woes. As Byron observed, all of life is not continual joy—it can't be. Mountain climbers spend difficult hours and days for a few minutes at the summit. You will have summits again. Just not involving drugs or alcohol. But not yet. Now you are climbing, breathing hard, your lungs burning. You'd like to stop, to go back downward, but you can't, because there is no back to go down to. The town you departed from is gone, swept away in the landslide that sent you scrambling. There is only forward now.

．

When the morning's freshness has been replaced by the weariness of midday, when the leg muscles quiver under the strain, the climb seems endless, and, suddenly, nothing will go quite as you wish — it is then that you must *not* hesitate.

Dag Hammarskjöld, *Markings*

．

I feel that perhaps the sorrow of these days will be revealed to me as having had their usefulness. The nature of this sorrow is bewildering. I seek some familiarity that eludes me; I want to go home and I have no home.

John Cheever, journal entry, 1980

．

I wish one could be sure the suffering had a loving side. The thought to look down some day, and see the crooked steps we came, from a safer place, must be a precious thing...

Emily Dickinson, letter to Louise Norcross, May 1862

．

The wise men teach us well to save ourselves from our treacherous appetites and to distinguish true wholesome pleasures from pleasures diluted and crisscrossed by pain.

Michel de Montaigne, "On Solitude"

•

Wanting to stop drinking and wanting to get out of trouble are two different things.

Paul Molloy, *Where Did Everybody Go?*

•

...a cure imposed by the authorities lacks conviction in the heart.

Keith Richards, *Life*

•

"Men's courses will foreshadow certain ends, to which, if persevered in, they must lead," said Scrooge. "But if the courses be departed from, the ends will change."

Charles Dickens, *A Christmas Carol*

4

•

At moments of departure and a change of life, people capable of reflecting on their actions usually get into a serious state of mind. At these moments they usually take stock of the past and make plans for the future.

Leo Tolstoy, *War and Peace*

•

He believed that he must, that he could and would recover the good things, the happy things, the easy tranquil things of life. He had made mistakes, but he could overlook these. He had been a fool, but that could be forgiven. The time wasted—must be relinquished. What else could one do about it? Things were too complex, but they might be reduced to simplicity again. Recovery was possible.

Saul Bellow, *Seize the Day*

•

It may be unfair, but what happens in a few days, sometimes even a single day, can change the course of a whole lifetime...

Khaled Hosseini, *The Kite Runner*

•

People don't like it when you change. Even if that change is making your life better, they don't like it because a little piece of them dies.

Ricky Gervais, tweet, October 11, 2013

•

The reawakening of one's senses (the first clear symptom of recovery) is accompanied by sneezes, yawns, sniffling and tears. Another sign: the poultry in the hen house opposite exasperated me and so did those pigeons which trot up and down the tin roof, their hands behind their backs. On the seventh day the crow of the cock pleased me. I am writing these notes between six and seven in the morning. With opium nothing exists before eleven o'clock.

Jean Cocteau, *Opium*

•

It having been a very fine clear frosty day — God send us more of them, for the warm weather all this winter makes us fear a sick summer.

But thanks be to God, since my leaving drinking of wine, I do find myself much better and to mind my business better and to spend less money, and less time lost in idle company.

Samuel Pepys, diary entry, January 26, 1662

•

Do what you can — and the task will rest lightly in your hand, so lightly that you will be able to look forward to the more difficult tests which may be awaiting you.

Dag Hammarskjöld, *Markings*

•

4

I . . . generally behaved myself — a sensation still having the charm of novelty.

Edith Wharton, letter, September 23, 1876

•

Not drinking is beginning to be refreshing. Still, it will be lonely in New York, unless you come. I've developed a craving for Welch's grape juice and gingerale and drink a large concentrated bottle each afternoon at the cocktail hour.

Robert Lowell, letter to Elizabeth Bishop, August 31, 1961

•

…I'm no longer crouched over the problem, looking furtively over my shoulder. I'm lurching forward in my life again, and it feels as if someone finally cracked open a window that had been jammed.

Anne Lamott, *Grace (Eventually)*

•

BOSWELL: The great difficulty of resisting wine is from benevolence. For instance, a good worthy man takes you to taste his wine, which he has had twenty years in his cellar.

JOHNSON: Sir, all this notion about benevolence arises from a man's imagining himself to be of more importance to others, than he really is. They don't care a farthing whether he drinks wine or not.

SIR JOSHUA REYNOLDS: Yes, they do for the time.

JOHNSON: For the time!—If they care this minute, they forget it the next. And as for the good worthy man; how do you know he is good and worthy? No good and worthy man will insist upon another man's drinking wine…I allow it is something to please one's company; and people are always pleased with those who partake pleasure with them. But after a man has brought himself to relinquish the great personal pleasure which arises from drinking wine, any other consideration is a trifle.

James Boswell, *The Life of Samuel Johnson*

•

For how does any man keep straight with himself if he has
no one with whom to be straight?

Nelson Algren, *The Man with the Golden Arm*

•

O! I have suffered
With those that I saw suffer.

William Shakespeare, *The Tempest*

•

I'd like to begin again. Not touch my
own face, not tremble in the dark before
an intruder who never arrives. Not
apologize. Not scurry, not pace. Not
refuse to keep notes of what meant the most.
Not skirt my father's ghost. Not abandon
piano, or a book before the end.
Not count, count, count and wait, poised—the control,
the agony controlled—for the loss of
the one, having borne. I can't be, won't breathe
without; the foregone conclusion, the pain
not yet met, the preemptive mourning
without which
          nothing left of me but smoke.

Deborah Garrison, "On New Terms"

•

That Christmas he and Lee traveled to Deep River, Connecticut, to spend a week with his family, and his mother soon reported exuberantly, "There was no drinking. We were all so happy...hope he will stay with it he says he wants to quit and went to the Dr. on his own."

Deborah Solomon, *Jackson Pollock*

•

You know, you never really saw me sober and I have been sober now for some weeks—absolutely bone-dry sober. Dull as it may be I intend to remain that way. Something in my chemistry will no longer accept alcohol. There is some sort of chain reaction. I start off with a drink of white wine and end up drinking two bottles of Scotch a day. Then I stop eating. I have to quit and the withdrawal symptoms are simply awful. I shake so that I can't hold a glass of water. One day I vomited eighteen times. My father was an alcoholic and I have lived my whole life in fear of becoming one but until my wife died I always quit drinking on my own power when I felt there was a real need for it.

Raymond Chandler, letter to
Jessica Tyndale, September 17, 1955

•

Up the river to Yaddo for the first time in many years without the company of alcohol.

John Cheever, journal entry, 1975

•

Besides, it is a certain fact that I have done better work than before since I stopped drinking, and that is so much gained.

Vincent van Gogh, letter to Mr. and Mrs. Ginoux, 1890

•

Bird himself was wary of the craving, occult but deeply rooted, that he still had for alcohol. Often since those four weeks in whisky hell he had asked himself why he had stayed drunk for seven hundred hours, and never had he arrived at a conclusive answer. So long as his descent into the abyss of whisky remained a riddle, there was a constant danger he might suddenly return.

Kenzaburō Ōe, *A Personal Matter*

•

How far back must you go to discover the beginning of trouble?

Philip Roth, "Epstein"

•

There are very few human beings who receive the truth, complete and staggering, by instant illumination. Most of them acquire it fragment by fragment, on a small scale, by successive developments, cellularly, like a laborious mosaic.

Anaïs Nin, diary entry, fall 1943

•

You were sick, but now you're well, and there's work to do.

Kurt Vonnegut, *Timequake*

•

Habit is habit, and not to be flung out of the window by any man, but coaxed down-stairs a step at a time.

Mark Twain, *Pudd'nhead Wilson's Calendar*

•

A month now has gone by without my drinking a drop. I feel on the side of life or something of the sort. I have a funny increased feeling of knowing, of watching each error and mis-step and wrong feeling as they happen.

Robert Lowell, letter to Elizabeth Bishop, July 5, 1963

•

To possess your soul in patience, with all the skin and some of the flesh burnt off your face and hands, is a job for a boy compared with the pains of a man who has lived pretty long in the exhilarating world that drugs or strong waters seem to create and is trying to live now in the first bald desolation created by knocking them off . . .

Charles Edward Montague, *Disenchantment*

•

You are never stronger . . . than when you land on the other side of despair.

Zadie Smith, *White Teeth*

•

I am withdrawing from the scourge of forty-five years of drinking. Two months ago I stumbled into a treatment center for alcohol and drug addiction. Now, I am barely detoxed. Standing here among the sword ferns my senses seem to be thin glass, so acute at their edges I am afraid I will cut myself simply by touching the silicon edge of a bamboo leaf.

Patrick Lane, *What the Stones Remember*

•

"Listen, Truman, it's the most terrible, glum place you can conceivably imagine. It's really, really, really grim. But I did come out of there sober, and I have been sober for two and a half years."

John Cheever, quoted in *Capote*

4

•

My identity shifted when I got into recovery. That's who I am now, and it actually gives me greater pleasure to have that identity than to be a musician or anything else, because it keeps me in a manageable size. When I'm down on the ground with my disease—which I'm happy to have—it gets me in tune. It gives me a spiritual anchor. Don't ask me to explain.

Eric Clapton, interview, *Esquire*, January 2008

•

In a time of drastic change one can be too preoccupied with what is ending or too obsessed with what seems to be beginning. In either case one loses touch with the present and with its obscure but dynamic possibilities. What really matters is openness, readiness, attention, courage to face risk. You do not need to know precisely what is happening, or exactly where it is all going. What you need is to recognize the possibilities and challenges offered by the present moment, and to embrace them with courage, faith, and hope.

Thomas Merton, *Conjectures of a Guilty Bystander*

•

... happiness is not something that happens. It is not the result of good fortune or random chance. It is not something that money can buy or power command. It does not depend on outside events, but, rather, on how we interpret them. Happiness, in fact, is a condition that must be prepared for, cultivated, and defended privately by each person. People who learn to control inner experience will be able to determine the quality of their lives, which is as close as any of us can come to being happy.

Mihaly Csikszentmihalyi, *Flow*

•

I no longer plumb the depths of despair. My sadness has become a springboard. In the past I used to think that I would always be sad, but now I know that those moments too are part of life's ebb and flow and that all is well. This is a sign of confidence, of very great confidence, even in myself. I have confidence in my own seriousness, and I have gradually come to realize that I am going to manage my life properly.

Etty Hillesum, diary entry, January 11, 1942

4

FIVE

WAIT, FOR NOW

The Importance of Time

Wait, for now.
Distrust everything if you have to.
But trust the hours. Haven't they
carried you everywhere, up to now?

Galway Kinnell, "Wait"

A key to recovery is time. Not having a drink this minute loses significance if you take a drink the next minute. You must not only resist temptation but resist it over time.

Maintaining sobriety becomes a blending of the immediate and the long term. You need to not only do the right thing *now*, but to continue doing it—today, this week, and over the future to come.

That is why people in recovery count the months, the years. An alcoholic resisting drink for an entire weekend, like Jack London avoiding booze on part of his ocean voyage, has not achieved the redemptive triumph he might consider his feat to be. But a month? A year? A decade? That's huge. Although, as they say in the investment business, past performance is no guarantee of future results.

Hence the difficulty. Because your enemy is relentless, and one slip-up, one crack in the wall, and it all can come rushing back. After bombing the Grand Hotel failed to kill British Prime Minister Margaret Thatcher, the Irish Republican Army sent her a message: "Today we were unlucky, but remember, we only have to be lucky once. You will have to be lucky always."

Nobody is lucky always. Which is why recovery is never an accidental process. Good fortune won't do it. Craving doesn't just go away, you have to make it go away, and central is the understanding that cravings pass. Just as the euphoria that first comes with quitting substance abuse fades, so the urge—the "I must!" that springs out of the subcellars of your mind—passes, if you keep the door bolted and wait for it to pass.

Or not to pass. This is the "powerlessness" that AA talks about. Your will crumples before your compulsion, again and again, until a moment of grace arrives and you find the strength to finally make sobriety stick, whether with the help of God and the fellow-ship of AA or buried within yourself, after you just get so sick of the whole thing that you finally tough it out.

However success comes, tamping down the craving is only the start—you need to fill the hours of your life with something you love, or used to love, or could love. Otherwise relapse will eventually become your only option, as the thing you most want to do in life reasserts its authority. This can initially sound a lot harder than it turns out to be. The world offers so many wonders that *aren't* drinking or drugs. An addict focuses on one thing, the adored substance, while the person in recovery is learning to focus on everything else, gradually understanding that making this swap—giving up one thing in return for everything else—is actually a pretty good deal, and only skewed addictive judgment would lead someone to believe otherwise.

Part of recovery is recovering the person you once were, the child within who was dulled by addiction. It is a sign of how overwhelming addiction is that at first anything can seem a paltry substitute: I'm supposed to keep sober by reading philosophy? By riding my bike? By knitting? By listening to music? By merely being alive?

Yes.

Then there is also the issue of dealing with a past so vivid it can feel like the present and come rushing back unexpectedly to torment you even though you're doing the right thing and walking the right path.

Vermont poet Galway Kinnell wrote "Wait" for a student contemplating suicide after a failed love affair. He points out that other loves will come, that interest in both small matters such as the state of your hair and great wonders such as nature will return. He encourages what is a central skill in recovery—the ability to hunker down, to endure. Sometimes it is referred to dismissively as "white knuckling"—an almost physical clinging to sobriety, eyes clenched, howling defiance, avoiding alcohol through force of will as opposed to the liberating spiritual epiphany outlined in AA's famous Twelve Steps. But if white knuckling is all you've got, do it. Because the reward is coming. Kinnell writes:

> Personal events will become interesting again.
> Hair will become interesting.
> Pain will become interesting.
> Buds that open out of season will become interesting.

You are becoming reacquainted with aspects of life that you turned away from to embrace addiction. They're unfamiliar and therefore, as is often the case with strange things, a little frightening, or at least off-putting. Here time is also an ally—give yourself a chance to become comfortable with regular living again, to settle into new routines that you will someday be unwilling to abandon. Building a life that nurtures and sustains you is the best defense against the lure of an existence that was undermining and destroying you. This process cannot be rushed; it unfolds at its own pace. If you are becoming sober at the insistence of someone else—a common occurrence—you will eventually realize, again in time, that you are actually doing this for yourself, or should be. You will also need to repair your relationships with the people around you, and that, too, is not something that can be rushed.

College wrestlers score points even when they don't pin their opponents, just for being in a superior position and holding on. Sobriety is no different. Your opponent is never pinned, the match is never over. It is enough to be in a good place and stay there. Sobriety has its rhythms, now easy, now hard. That is another reason why people in recovery count their days, their weeks, their years. Even if none of this makes sense, even if you have not found the things in life that are going to carry you forward, even if you see a drink in the hand of every person in every photograph, even if you reflexively scrutinize every clear plastic baggie you notice blowing down the street to see if there are drugs inside, you are still building your sober life.

"Time off the drug," said Walter Ling, director of the Integrated Substance Abuse Programs at UCLA, "is the best predictor of more time off the drug." Underline "predictor" as opposed to "guarantee." In recovery, nothing is guaranteed. Sometimes being clean for a long time means you've left your using days safely behind; sometimes it means you're already forgetting what you overcame and are prone to stumble.

Which option turns out to be true is up to you. Whether you know it or not, changes are going on inside you. You weren't born an addict but drifted gradually into addiction over a long period—it could take an equally long period for you to climb your way out. Or wait your way out. You are not going to die but live, and living requires a change in essential perspective, and that change takes time.

You can combat your craving thoughts with what psychologists call metathinking, a practical mental tool that allows you to deflect destructive impulses. If your whole self wants to run to the liquor store, you can form a metathought that looks down on that compulsion, recognizes it, and responds: "No. I'm not doing that. I *want* to do that now, part of me does, the old part, but if I don't do it, and wait, the desire will pass, and I'll be far better off than had I let this obsession guide me."

The moment you realize that, you are halfway to prevailing over your urges. To return to Kinnell's poem:

> Wait.
> Don't go too early.
> You're tired. But everyone's tired.

But no one is tired enough.
Only wait a little and listen:
music of hair,
music of pain,
music of looms weaving all our loves again.
Be there to hear it . . .

•

Life is very long

T. S. Eliot, "The Hollow Men"

•

Barflies mortgage years to buy hours.

Michael Miner, *Chicago Reader*

•

Saturday   *17th* Sunned, read, biked.
      Sunday, 18th Booze.
      Monday, 19th Booze.
      Tuesday, 20th Booze.
      Wednesday 21st Booze.
      Thursday 22nd. Booze.
      Friday 23rd Booze.
      Saturday 24th Went into clinic late afternoon.
      Sunday 25th Tests and books.
      Monday 26th More tests hate clinics.
      Tuesday 27th Home from *three* day check-up in clinic. OK everywhere except for slightly enlarged liver. No wonder.

Richard Burton, diary entry, May 1975

•

The events in our lives happen in a sequence in time, but in their significance to ourselves they find their own order, a timetable not necessarily—perhaps not possibly—chronological. The time as we know it subjectively is often the chronology that stories and novels follow: it is the continuous thread of revelation.

Eudora Welty, *One Writer's Beginnings*

•

The blizzard doesn't last forever; it just seems so.

Ray Bradbury, *Snoopy's Guide to the Writing Life*

•

POZZO: [*suddenly furious*]. Have you not done tormenting me with your accursed time! It's abominable! When! When! One day, is that not enough for you, one day he went dumb, one day I went blind, one day we'll go deaf, one day we were born, one day we shall die, the same day, the same second, is that not enough for you? [*Calmer.*] They give birth astride of a grave, the light gleams an instant, then it's night once more.

Samuel Beckett, *Waiting for Godot*

•

For only you could watch yourself so patiently from afar
The way God watches a sinner on the path to redemption,
Sometimes disappearing into valleys, but always *on the
    way,*
For it all builds up into something, meaningless or
    meaningful
As architecture, because planned and then abandoned
    when completed,
To live afterwards, in sunlight and shadow, a certain
    amount of years.

Who cares about what was there before? There is no
   going back,
For standing still means death, and life is moving on,
Moving on toward death. But sometimes standing still is
   also life.

John Ashbery, "The Bungalows"

•

With alcohol it was decompression. The same way I started drinking, I stopped. You work your way down the ladder from Jack Daniel's to mixed drinks to wine to wine coolers and finally to Perrier. With cocaine, there is no way to gently decompress yourself. It took a few months. Someone said you finally realize you've kicked cocaine when you no longer talk about it. Then it's gone. It's like pulling away and seeing Pittsburgh from the air.

Robin Williams, interview, *Rolling Stone*

•

What wound did ever heal but by degrees?

William Shakespeare, *Othello*

•

The solution is not to suppress our thoughts and desires, for this would be impossible; it would be like trying to keep a pot of water from boiling by pressing down tightly on the lid. The only sensible approach is to train ourselves to observe our thoughts without following them. This deprives them of their compulsive energy and is therefore like removing the pot of boiling water from the fire.

Thubten Yeshe, *Introduction to Tantra*

•

For me there was a real repulsion at the beginning. "One Day at a Time," right? I'm thinking 1977, Norman Lear, starring Bonnie Franklin. Show me the needlepointed sampler this is written on. But apparently part of addiction is that you need the substance so bad that when they take it away from you, you want to die. And it's so awful that the only way to deal with it is to build a wall at midnight and not look over it. Something as banal and reductive as "One Day at a Time" enabled these people to walk through hell, which from what I could see the first six months of detox is.

David Foster Wallace, interview, *Salon*

•

5

Sign on to a process and see where it takes you. You don't have to invent the wheel every day. Today you'll do what you did yesterday, tomorrow you'll do what you did today. Eventually you'll get somewhere.

Chuck Close, "Note to Self"

•

In a dark time, the eye begins to see,
I meet my shadow in the deepening shade;
I hear my echo in the echoing wood —
A lord of nature weeping to a tree.

Theodore Roethke, "In a Dark Time"

•

The brave are patient.
They are the priests of sunrise,
lions on the ramparts, the promontory.

Louise Glück, "From the Japanese"

•

Let everything happen to you: beauty and terror.
Only press on: no feeling is final.

Rainer Maria Rilke, *Book of Hours*

•

Be of good hope. Try to think in terms of "the long run"
and store up your honey like the bees.

May Sarton, letter to Madeleine L'Engle, July 18, 1954

•

There are mountainous, arduous days, up which one takes
an infinite time to climb, and downward-sloping days
which one can descend at full tilt, singing as one goes.

Marcel Proust, *Remembrance of Things Past*

•

I keep crying out to myself: "Count your years, and you
will be ashamed to desire and pursue the same things you
desired in your boyhood days. Of this one thing make sure

against your dying day—let your faults die before you die. Away with those disordered pleasures, which must be dearly paid for."

Seneca, Epistle 27

.

Time will say nothing but I told you so.

W. H. Auden, "If I Could Tell You"

.

Longevity is more fun than the drugs.

Steve Van Zandt, interview, *New Yorker*

.

5

The first three or four months I think is the hardest. When you don't have a pattern of behavior, you don't really know what to do with yourself. But after that it got a whole lot easier. You know, you get a lot more hours out of the day.

Jason Isbell, interview, *Huffington Post*

.

So, a full year is coming. I am beginning to enjoy not drinking and am almost vain about it—what a change from last fall, with its mania followed by gloom.

Robert Lowell, letter to Elizabeth Bishop, September 11, 1963

•

To have a problem in common is much like love and that kind of love was often the bread that we broke among us. And some of us survived and some of us didn't, and it was sometimes a matter of what's called luck and sometimes a matter of having or not having the gift to endure and the will to.

Tennessee Williams, *Memoirs*

•

There's something about sober living and sober thinking, about facing long afternoons without the numbing distraction of anesthesia, that disabuses you of the belief in externals, shows you that strength and hope come not from circumstances or the acquisition of things but from the simple accumulation of active experience, from gritting the teeth and checking the items off the list, one by one, even though it's painful and you're afraid.

Caroline Knapp, *Drinking*

•

It was a weekday afternoon, around three,
the hour some drinkers call the Demon,
and I was possessed by the feeling

that nothing had really changed for me
since childhood,
that I was spinning my wheels in a sandbox

Billy Collins, "Scotland"

•

I miss drinking. That's the simplest way of putting it. When it grows dark I would like a drink.

John Cheever, journal entry, 1980

•

It was humid in here, but it was more than the humidity that brought the sick and slimy sweat onto his brow and stomach and legs. The remembering did that, it was a total thing that made that night two years ago seem like two hours ago. There was no lag. It brought the shame and re-vulsion back, the sense of having no worth at all, and that feeling always made him want to have a drink, and the wanting of a drink brought still blacker despair — would he ever have an hour, not a week or even a day, mind you, but just one waking hour when the craving for a drink wouldn't surprise him like this?

Stephen King, *The Shining*

•

It is time now, I said,
for the deepening and quieting of the spirit
among the flux of happenings.

Something had pestered me so much
I thought my heart would break.
I mean, the mechanical part.

I went down in the afternoon
to the sea
which held me, until I grew easy.

About tomorrow, who knows anything.
Except that it will be time, again,
for the deepening and quieting of the spirit.

Mary Oliver, "Swimming, One Day in August"

•

Master of beauty, craftsman of the snowflake,
inimitable contriver,
endower of Earth so gorgeous & different from the
    boring Moon,
thank you for such as it is my gift.

.   .   .   .

You have come to my rescue again & again
in my impassable, sometimes despairing years.
You have allowed my brilliant friends to destroy
    themselves
and I am still here, severely damaged, but functioning.

.   .   .   .

Sole watchman of the flying stars, guard me
against my flicker of impulse lust: teach me
to see them as sisters & daughters. Sustain
my grand endeavours: husbandship & crafting.

Forsake me not when my wild hours come;
grant me sleep nightly, grace softens my dreams;
achieve in me patience till the thing be done,
a careful view of my achievement come.

Make me from time to time the gift of the shoulder.
When all hurt nerves whine shut away the whiskey.
Empty my heart toward Thee.
Let me pace without fear the common path of death.

.   .   .   .

Ease in their passing my beloved friends,
all others too I have cared for in a traveling life,
anyone anywhere indeed. Lift up
sober toward truth a scared self-estimate.

.   .   .   .

Fearful I peer upon the mountain path
where once Your shadow passed. Limner of the clouds
up their phantastic guesses. I am afraid,
I never until now confessed.

5

I fell back in love with you, Father, for two reasons:
You were good to me, & a delicious author.

John Berryman, "Eleven Addresses to the Lord"

.

Shall we say that there are times when thirsty people are
not willing to drink?

— Certainly it happens often and to many people.

What then, I said, should one say about this? Is there
not in their soul that which bids them drink, and also that
which prevents them, that the latter is different and over-
rules the other part?

— I think so, he said.

And the preventing part comes into play as a result of
reasoning, whereas the impulses that lead and drag him are
due to emotive states and diseases?

—Apparently.

It is therefore not unreasonable for us to say that there are two distinct parts, to call that with which it reasons the rational part of the soul, and that with which it lusts and feels hungry and thirsty and gets excited with other desires the irrational and appetitive part, the companion of repletions and pleasures.

—That is the natural way for us to think.

Let these two then be described as two parts existing in the soul.

Plato, *The Republic*

•

...a man that drinks is two people, one grabbing the bottle, the other one fighting him off it, not one but two people fighting each other to get control of a bottle.

Tennessee Williams, *Three Players of a Summer Game*

•

...pride and drug addiction are forever at odds. If pride wins, the person escapes the tragedy of addiction, while gaining an understanding of human frailty at its most harrowing. If addiction wins, however, pride takes that hard, mutating fall, boiling away in the bent spoon where the dope is cooked.

Stanley Crouch, *Kansas City Lightning*

•

Many dubious and troublesome things are still in store for me. What I used to love, I love no longer. But I lie: I love it still, but less passionately. Again have I lied: I love it, but more timidly, more sadly. Now at last I have told the truth; for thus it is: I love, but what I should love not to love, what I should wish to hate. Nevertheless I love it, but against my will, under compulsion and in sorrow and mourning. To my own misfortune I experience in myself now the meaning of that most famous line: "Hate I shall, if I can; if I can't, I shall love though not willing." The third year has not yet elapsed since that perverted and malicious will, which had totally seized me and reigned in the court of my heart without an opponent, began to encounter a rebel offering resistance. A stubborn and still undecided battle has been long raging on the field of my thoughts for the supremacy of one of the two men within me.

Petrarch, *The Ascent of Mount Ventoux*

•

5

I am being driven forward
Into an unknown land.
The pass grows steeper,
The air colder and sharper.
A wind from my unknown goal
Stirs the strings
Of expectation.

Still the question:
Shall I ever get there?
There where life resounds,
A clear pure note
In the silence.

Dag Hammarskjöld, "Thus it was"

•

⋇ To bear is to conquer our fate.

Thomas Campbell, "Lines Written on
Visiting a Scene in Argyleshire"

•

Call up your courage again. Dismiss your grief and fear.
A joy it will be one day, perhaps, to remember even this.
Through so many hard straits, so many twists and turns
our course holds firm for Latium. There Fate holds out
a homeland, calm, at peace. There the gods decree
the kingdom of Troy will rise again. Bear up.
Save your strength for better times to come.

Virgil, *The Aeneid*

•

...unfortunately, it's true: time does heal. It will do so
whether you like it or not, and there's nothing anyone can
do about it. If you're not careful, time will take away everything that ever hurt you, everything you have ever lost, and
replace it with knowledge. Time is a machine: it will convert your pain into experience. Raw data will be compiled,
will be translated into a more comprehensible language.
The individual events of your life will be transmuted into
another substance called memory and in the mechanism
something will be lost and you will never be able to reverse
it, you will never again have the original moment back in
its uncategorized, preprocessed state. It will force you to
move on and you will not have a choice in the matter.

Charles Yu, *How to Live Safely in a Science Fictional Universe*

•

The past is gone. I know that. The future isn't here yet,
whatever it's going to be. So all there is is this, the present.
That's it.

Jim Jarmusch, *Broken Flowers*

•

It is sometimes so bitterly cold in the winter that one says,
"The cold is too awful for me to care whether summer is
coming or not; the harm outdoes the good." But with or
without our approval, the severe weather does come to an
end eventually and one fine morning the wind changes and
there is the thaw. When I compare the state of the weather
to our state of mind and our circumstances, subject to
change and fluctuation like the weather, then I still have
some hope that things may get better.

Vincent van Gogh, letter to his brother Theo, August 1879

•

Enormous or not, life is made of small things, small happi-
nesses chained like daisies, one by one. Let the next year
be such a chain for you.

Vincent Hepp, Christmas message to May Sarton

•

Who knows what the day after tomorrow will bring—the
very thing we most wanted and haven't allowed our hearts
to hope.

William Maxwell, letter to Eudora Welty, January 24, 1967

SIX

SOME-WHERE TO GO

Alcoholics Anonymous

For every man must have somewhere to go. Since there are times when one absolutely must go somewhere!

Fyodor Dostoevsky, *Crime and Punishment*

You are probably not a drunk like Marmeladov, the clerk in *Crime and Punishment*. Slumped in a tavern at the end of a five-day binge, filthy, with bits of straw from the hay barge he's been sleeping in at night stuck to him. He begins to harangue Raskolnikov about his miserable existence, particularly about his refined, long-suffering wife.

"Do you know, sir, do you know, I have sold her very stockings for drink?" Marmeladov asks. "Her mohair shawl I sold for drink, a present to her long ago, her own property, not mine; and we live in a cold room..."

Let's hope you aren't like him. Though maybe you are. Maybe you are worse, or on your way to worse. That will depend on whether you resist your addiction or surrender to it and, ironically, the impulse that Marmeladov blames for driving him to the tavern also drives many toward eventual salvation.

He doesn't cite the chemical lure of alcohol, but the need to escape the silent rebuke of his three hungry children and the hair-pulling reproach of his plundered, tubercular wife. He can't bear being at home.

"Do you understand, sir, do you understand what it means when you have absolutely nowhere to turn?" Marmeladov says, explaining his flight toward the taproom. "You know every man ought to have at least one place where people feel for him!"

Indeed we do. For the drinker, that is the bar, for the addict, the drug house, the needle park. And for the person new to sobriety, ready to turn away from old haunts, that place is often AA—Alcoholics Anonymous, the bedrock where people knowledgeable and sympathetic to his or her condition are always waiting, ready to listen, the international network of mutual aid founded in an Akron, Ohio, hotel in 1935 by Bill Wilson and Dr. Bob Smith.

What is AA? A loose affiliation of small groups—AA reports there are more than a hundred thousand around the world—made up of those who wish to keep sober by following the twelve steps to recovery set down by Wilson and Smith, which begin: "1. We admitted we were powerless over alcohol—that our lives had become unmanageable" and declare that a "Power greater than ourselves could restore us to sanity." The steps guide alcoholics to apologize and make amends to those harmed during their years of addiction and toward a "spiritual awakening" that permits a sober life dedicated to helping others.

You do not have to join or pay or even give your name—in fact, last names are discouraged. You do not have to dress nicely or make an appointment. You just show up, and everyone from movie stars to Marmeladovs comes to AA, often at the same meeting. All are welcome.

Meetings—sometimes limited to an hour—often begin with a prayer, and include readings from the AA list of canonical works, particularly *The Big Book*, AA's bible of personal tales of suffering and redemption. Often there is a main speaker, followed by a chance for everyone present to talk about his or her life, a brief monologue that typically begins, "Hello, I'm . . ." and then the speaker's first name, "and I'm an alcoholic." That can be a powerful moment, admitting the truth, since so many refuse to acknowledge it even to themselves, never mind in public, and because recognizing the problem is the crucial first step in doing something about it. You don't have to say that—you don't have to say anything. You can smile and pass when your turn comes. Sometimes it takes a while to gather your courage.

Alcoholics Anonymous costs nothing, though those able to do so contribute a few dollars to pay for coffee and the room. In any big city, there are meetings throughout the day, early in the morning, at lunch, in the evening. Groups vary in size, but a typical meeting will have a couple dozen people. There are specialized meetings directed toward particular populations—some meetings are only for women, or atheists, or specifically aimed toward drug users: Narcotics Anonymous, or NA. There is also Al-Anon for the families of alcoholics, who learn to step away, protect themselves, and not be drawn into the perpetual drama and ongoing chaos of addiction.

Odds are if you are not becoming sober of your own volition—the common situation—you will start attending AA either because your spouse or boss or family demands that you go or because whatever rehab center you find yourself in requires that you attend meetings. Sometimes a court orders you to go. Hence a certain resentment may be associated with a person's introduction to AA, as with all mandatory activities. Views of AA range from undiluted and enthusiastic love and support, as the one essential pillar on which to build a successful sober life, to open condemnation, even contempt, dismissing AA as a church or a cult, a 1930s relic to be avoided at all costs. While many in AA strenuously discount the religious aspect of the program, five of the twelve steps mention "God" and that can be troublesome for those who don't see why they can't get sober without divine assistance. Others easily ignore that element and take what helps them. Some credit AA for saving their lives. Some try it and find it lacking. Some would rather die than go to AA. Some do.

There are those who attend AA for years. Others find that AA is helpful in the crisis of early recovery but eventually drift away, maintaining sobriety on their own terms.

Where you fit on that continuum depends on you.

However you view the program, as it is known (they take the anonymous part very seriously), it involves not only mastering the AA literature and working the steps, with the help of a more-experienced AA sponsor, but also talking about yourself—and here Dostoevsky offers an interesting perspective. Telling one's tale, and hearing the tales of others, are considered key to forming the mental framework to keep sober. You realize that your situation is not unique and learn from the "experience, strength, and hope" of others. Those who can't yet admit to being alcoholics attend meetings and realize their true situation through a simple syllogism: (*A*) These people are obviously alcoholics; (*B*) My life is just like theirs; therefore, (*C*) I'm an alcoholic, too.

But Dostoevsky sees the confessional conversation of Marmeladov not as redemptive but as merely a barfly's inclination, indulged in drunk or sober.

"He had most likely acquired his weakness for high-flown speeches from the habit of frequently entering into conversation with strangers of all sorts in the tavern," Dostoevsky notes. "This habit develops into a necessity in some drunkards, and especially in those who are looked after sharply and kept in order at home. Hence in the company of other drinkers they try to justify themselves . . ."

And that is one of the questions to consider as you approach AA—are you attempting to change yourself, or merely to justify yourself? Because the qualities of AA that may initially seem off-putting eventually may be viewed in a new, very different light if you stick with it. One reason AA is so hard, at first, is that it tears down your glib self-justifications. That's the main purpose of going. So don't let the mirror being held up, or minor considerations such as the setting, throw you. Yes, the meetings are generally held in church basements and assorted odd places. Your fellow drunks do not always offer a tableau of humanity that you will immediately enjoy including yourself among. Whatever accomplishments and distinctions you fancy make you extraordinary mean nothing in AA. We all are level, all equal, all identical in our problems, brothers and sisters on this journey along the same road using the same techniques to head toward the same coveted destination. That is not a philosophy everyone is willing to immediately embrace, particularly those who are more interested in defending their personality than altering it. They recoil at the thought of being exactly like everybody else, even in just this one regard, by participating in a system designed for anyone who walks in the door.

In AA, it is not justification that is sought but humility, surrender, and acceptance. Finding a "higher power" and seeking out the fellowship of other alcoholics bring exactly that for millions, but the process demands, as AA continually points out—and repetition is a hallmark of the program—a rigorous honesty, to explain what has happened in order to comprehend it and find a new way to live. To help yourself and, by doing so, help others; and to help others and, in doing so, help yourself. To take something that drunks often keep secret—their problem and the terrible things it often compels them to do—and drag it into the open, into the light, in this safe environment. Nothing is guaranteed. There is controversy over how well AA works and whether twelve-step programs should occupy the central place they do in recovery. You may use AA to gain sobriety, but then not want to spend your new life at AA meetings, although some would say that is setting yourself up for relapse.

But even the most broken drunk, marinated in the deceits that come with addiction, selling his sick wife's warm clothing for booze, watching his daughter drift into prostitution, realizes that honesty and acceptance are key to grasping this obsession.

"All that is secret is made open," Marmeladov says. "And I accept it all, not with contempt, but with humility."

•

They say if you get far enough away
you'll be on your way back home.

Tom Waits, "Blind Love"

•

It may be that when we no longer know what to do, we
have come to our real work, and that when we no longer
know which way to go, we have begun our real journey.
The mind that is not baffled is not employed. The impeded
stream is the one that sings.

Wendell Berry, "Marriage, Too,
May Have Something to Teach Us"

•

Think of it like a date. Just go to dinner and see if it works.
If you go to a bad movie, you're out ten bucks and an evening. If you go to an AA meeting and don't like it you're
only out an evening. Give it a go. See if any of it sticks.

Dr. Keith Humphreys, Stanford University

•

But is waiting forever
always the answer? Nothing
is always the answer; the answer
depends on the story.

Such a mistake to want
clarity above all things. What's
a single night, especially
one like this, now so close to ending?
On the other side, there could be anything,
all the joy in the world, the stars fading,
the streetlight becoming a bus stop.

Louise Glück, "Moonless Night"

·

My father had always been wary of Alcoholics Anonymous. He referred to its members as "a bunch of Christers." Before he would allow himself to be checked in at the alcohol and drug treatment center where he finally dried out for good, he phoned my sister and asked her to call the place and make absolutely sure that their program had no affiliation with AA. She called the clinic and then phoned him back to say there was no connection. This was a lie, but he would say later that it had saved his life.

Benjamin Cheever, *The Letters of John Cheever*

·

From a certain point on, there is no more turning back. That is the point that must be reached.

Franz Kafka, *The Zürau Aphorisms*

·

The Texas beauties each take turns telling their stories. To my amazement, most of them talk about *gratitude*, how different their lives are now without alcohol, how hard they've worked and continue to work so that they never return to their old ways. I'm trying to imagine any of them doing or saying or even witnessing the things I've done, said, and seen. I want to shrivel up and die. I want to go across the street and drink in that grotto bar. I want . . . so much.

Suddenly, it's my turn.

"Hi," I say. "I'm here because I'm twenty-nine years old and I can't remember the last time I went more than a day without drinking. I drink until I black out around five nights a week. I drink as much when I'm happy as when I'm sad. I drink when I'm frustrated, curious, anxious, scared . . . I drink when I'm really just hungry. I drink in the morning, which is considered a low point for some people, though I don't understand why. It's actually the best time of day to drink — nothing bad has happened yet. I drink at lunchtime to get myself ready to write. I drink in the afternoon either to reward myself for a job well done or to console myself for another wasted, unproductive day. I drink at night because it's dark out. I drink all the time, often alone. Here's the strange part — sometimes, I'm not joking, *I drink by accident.* I'll be out walking, ruminating, and suddenly I'll come to, like out of a trance, and find myself at the corner store, in the wine aisle. There is a bottle of Chianti, right in front of me. There it is, in my hand. I'll pretend I'm reading the label, but who am I trying to kid? I don't know anything about wine. All I see is the price tag and the picture. For eighteen bucks, a bird in the silhouette of a gibbous moon. For a bullfighter, only twelve. A castle is $7.99. What's weird is that I didn't even mean to buy booze today. In fact, I swore, when I woke up in the morning, that I wouldn't. Then I end up buying two bottles because they're on sale. Because one is never enough. I go home and finish the first bottle in under an hour, get all sentimental and depressed. I'll try to remember what my mother's voice sounds like. Then I'll remember and open the second bottle and try to forget.

"The worst part, I'm realizing, is that my drinking has nothing to do with her. She's not refilling my glass. I am.

"I always have a hangover. They get worse and worse. I puke so much, if I were a dog, I swear, my owners would have me put to sleep. Every year, since I can't remember when, I have tried to stop drinking. Just a month, I tell myself. To cleanse my liver. Always the month of February, because it's the shortest. But I never make it for more than a week or two. I can't.

"Now I'm done with all that. It's over. I'm ready to stop."

But I don't say any of that. Not yet.

"Hi" is what I actually say to them. Then tearfully, stupidly, "Um, hi."

For this I get what appears to be a silver poker chip, half a dozen unsolicited phone numbers, and a thunderous round of applause.

Domenica Ruta, *With or Without You*

·

meanwhile in my head
I'm undergoing open-heart surgery.

Anne Sexton, "Red Riding Hood"

·

To be confirmed in an enormous and splendid basilica, deafened by music and blinded by the fire of candles is much easier than it is to say in a smoke-filled Sunday

school classroom that my name is John and I am an alcoholic although they are the same thing.

John Cheever, papers in the
Berg Collection, New York Public Library

•

There was fear involved — yes — some
fear and hesitancy to discuss what
you knew you had done but
had not yet told anyone   It
was nothing   You discussed it for
hours — all that nothing and what
nothing meant . . .

                              It kept going
into itself and back out again
around the day — winding itself through
you and whispering things concerning you
across the wire and in sleep's
abysmal strangle and after all that
talk you felt true   Like a
new version of yourself you never
knew   A version of the very
dreadful nothing that you had always
had a vision of yourself becoming

Caryl Pagel, "Telephone"

•

But nothing disturbs the feeling of specialness like the
presence of other human beings feeling identically special.

Jonathan Franzen, *Freedom*

•

...lost among these entirely strange people.

Franz Kafka, diary entry, July 6, 1912

•

"And I myself am one of these.
For that defect alone our place is here."

Dante Alighieri, *Inferno*

•

6

It was terrifying to realize that I had to figure out what I actually liked to do. I had no ideas at first. And it seemed like I was surrounded by people who knew exactly who they were. Suddenly it became hard to contribute to conversations. I didn't have my salve to pave the way for clever thoughts—or to make me not care if what I said wasn't really clever.

Sacha Z. Scoblic, interview, *Time*

•

Now that my ladder's gone,
I must lie down where all the ladders start
In the foul rag and bone shop of the heart.

W. B. Yeats, "The Circus Animals' Desertion"

•

The mind must
set itself up
wherever it goes
and it would be
most convenient
to impose its
old rooms — just
tack them up
like an interior
tent. Oh but
the new holes
aren't where
the windows
went.

Kay Ryan, "New Rooms"

•

I did not know it was possible to be so miserable & live but
I am told that this is a common experience.

Evelyn Waugh, letter to Harold Acton, 1929

•

I want to tear myself from this place, from this reality, rise
up like a cloud and float away, melt into this humid summer night and dissolve somewhere far, over the hills. But I
am here, my legs blocks of concrete, my lungs empty of air,
my throat burning. There will be no floating away.

Khaled Hosseini, *The Kite Runner*

•

Don't pick up a drink or drug, one day at a time. It sounds so simple. It actually is simple but it isn't easy: it requires incredible support and fastidious structuring. Not to mention that the whole infrastructure of abstinence based recovery is shrouded in necessary secrecy. There are support fellowships that are easy to find and open to anyone who needs them but they eschew promotion of any kind in order to preserve the purity of their purpose, which is for people with alcoholism and addiction to help one another stay clean and sober.

6

Russell Brand, "My Life without Drugs"

•

One day at a time, sweet Jesus. Whoever wrote that one hadn't a clue. A day is a fuckin' eternity.

Roddy Doyle, *Paula Spencer*

•

Sometimes an abyss opens between Tuesday and Wednesday but twenty-six years could pass in a moment. Time is not a straight line, it's more of a labyrinth, and if you press close to the wall at the right place you can hear the hurrying steps and the voices, you can hear yourself walking past on the other side.

Tomas Tranströmer, "Answers to Letters"

•

"Fake it till you make it" someone will say, or "One day at a time," or "Stay out of using places and using faces." Give me a break. Here I am a goddamn published poet who has been ignored in several countries in the Western world and translated into Serbo-Croatian and left out of several of the best anthologies and I've got to listen to rhymes like these? "Walk the walk and talk the talk." "The past is history, the future's a mystery." Or some quirky little alliterative like "Let Go Let God." As if we ever let go of anything without leaving claw marks in it. And God? This Higher Power business? Why can't they just settle on a name like any other bunch? Yahweh or Jehovah or Jesus or Steve? And what about these little acronyms, like KISS (Keep It Simple Stupid), or don't get HALT (Hungry Angry Lonely or Tired)! How is a guy who's always been TBBTO (The Brains Behind the Operation) supposed to take such things seriously? Because even when they tell me it's a simple program for complex people, I think there must be more to it than that; more to it than some old-timer grinning at a table and holding up his thumb, saying "Don't take a drink," and then, on his index finger, "Go to meetings." Just two things? That's it? Give me a break. What's a guy who's read Dante and Pushkin need with meetings and head cases, and what does it mean when these nuts begin to make sense to him? And why can't it be like riding a bike—once you've got it you won't ever forget it? Though I've quit drinking like a drunk, I'm still inclined to thinking like one. Hear that little rhyme in there? And there's always this blathering idiot in my ear saying I can toss a few back like any normal guy, like eight out of ten of my fellow citizens, for whom enough is enough. What harm would it do? And the only thing between me and believing that voice and following its instructions are the men and women I meet with regularly who help me to remember the way I was.

Thomas Lynch, "The Way We Are"

•

Everyone thinks their own situation most tragic. I am no exception.

Jeanette Winterson, *Oranges Are Not the Only Fruit*

6

•

Every man, knowing to the smallest detail all the complexity of the conditions surrounding him, involuntarily assumes that the complexity of these conditions and the difficulty of comprehending them are only his personal, accidental peculiarity, and never thinks that others are surrounded by the same complexity as he is.

Leo Tolstoy, *Anna Karenina*

•

We are disclosing animals, wired for unburdening. It's what we do as a species.

David Rakoff, *Half Empty*

•

The relentlessly confessional tone of AA certainly did not suit his reserved Dutch nature. "There were the funniest stories of Bill in AA," said Joan. "He went to Montauk, where the people weren't all that rigid. He finally said, 'You people sure can beat a dead horse.' They thought that was very funny."

Mark Stevens and Annalyn Swan, *de Kooning*

•

"Everybody's story is the same," Humble Howard liked to say. "We drank too much, we came here, we stopped, and here we are to tell the tale." Before I went to my first meeting, I imagined the drunks would sit around telling drinking stories. Or perhaps they would all be depressing and solemn and holier-than-thou. I found out you rarely get to be an alcoholic by being depressing and solemn and holier-than-thou. These were the same people I drank with, although now they were making more sense.

Roger Ebert, "My Name Is Roger, and I'm an Alcoholic"

•

Their reward for enduring the awful experience was the right to tell people about it.

J. K. Rowling, *The Casual Vacancy*

•

A.A. is the world's largest functioning anarchy, and on the whole it performs astonishingly well.

Clancy Martin, "The Drunk's Club"

•

I telephoned my AA sponsor, Liquor Store Dave, from the coin phone in the upper hallway. In AA a "sponsor" is your support system, someone who has already worked the Twelve Steps and has been sober a while. Liquor Store Dave had dozens of recovering alkie friends. . . . He made me endure a five-minutes sponsor lecture. In the end, he insisted that I be willing to surrender to his advice. "You can't think your way into right acting, Bruno. You have to act your way into right thinking. Your Higher Power has to be your top priority. Recovery first, right?"

Dan Fante, *Mooch*

6

•

When we had reached the crag's high upper ledge,
out on the open hillside, 'Master,' I said,
'which path shall we take?'

And he to me: 'Do not fall back a single step.
Just keep climbing up behind me
until some guide who knows the way appears.'

The summit was so high that it was out of sight,
the slope far steeper than the line
drawn from midquadrant to the center.

Exhausted, I complained:
'Beloved father, turn around and see
how I'll be left alone unless you pause.'

'My son,' he said, 'drag yourself up there,'
pointing to a ledge a little higher,
which from that place encircles all the hill.

His words so spurred me on
I forced myself to clamber up
until I stood upon the ledge.

There we settled down to rest, facing
the east, where we had begun our climb,
for often it pleases us to see how far we've come.

Dante Alighieri, *Purgatorio*

•

The tasks that have been entrusted to us are often difficult.
Almost everything that matters is difficult, and everything
matters.

Rainer Maria Rilke, *Letters to a Young Poet*

•

I will leave here soon. I will go to Alcoholics Anonymous
meetings daily, sometimes more. I will sit under fluores-
cent lights and drink bad coffee, and I will listen to a great
deal of people talk about gratitude. Gratitude is a big part
of AA, and a favorite discussion topic of its adherents.
Gratitude to the program, to friends and family members,
to God—to God most of all; AA is a spiritual program before it's anything else. I will hear much talk of gratitude,
and I'll often try to feel some myself, though it won't come
easily. Because I won't like AA—won't like the coffee, the
lights, the clammy, feel-good spirituality, or the program's

tacit hostility toward the intellect. Some people love the program, but I will not.

Ben Zitsman, "Dispatches from Suspension"

•

A few months after I returned to New York from Paris, I finally, against all the resistance of my pride, attended a Narcotics Anonymous meeting. Beautiful Victoria, a sometime girlfriend I'd known since the early CBGB days, had cleaned up in NA and she persisted in urging me to try it. I fled the first meeting I attended, horrified that a stranger had approached me part of the way through and hugged me. On Victoria's reassurances, and for lack of any better ideas, I eventually tried again. On the second or third meeting, it took. I came to see the practicality of NA and I stayed with it, and I left music at the same time, knowing how pervasive and tempting drugs were in that line of work. There was a two-or-three year period of relapse at the end of the eighties and in the earliest nineties, but apart from that, I've had no drug problem since.

Richard Hell, *I Dreamed I Was a Very Clean Tramp*

•

All I wanted to do was to stay home and sit on the couch necking with my fear and depression. But I made myself show up, and it got me unstuck. Like they say, take the action and the insight will follow. There's still real life going on out there, and it was such a nice break to take my extension cord and plug into it for a while.

Anne Lamott, *Operating Instructions*

•

I used to be a boozer, but I gave it up. I don't miss it; never want one. I loved the AA meetings. I mean it was the same old stories each time but it was good to laugh about our situation...everyone was in the same boat together. We saw the humor in our predicament.

Willem de Kooning, *de Kooning and Me*

•

God bless the busted boat that brings us back.

Jason Isbell, "New South Wales"

•

Suddenly the cherries were there
although I had forgotten
that cherries exist

Günter Grass, "Transformation"

•

My wife insisted that I confine myself to a hospital for clinical alcoholics and I did. I came out of this prison 20 pounds lighter and howling with pleasure. That was a month ago and I'm still howling. I howl, write, dance, swim, eat, drink (tea only) and am terribly kind and patient to all dogs and children...

John Cheever, letter to Tanya Litvinov, 1975

•

O wonder!
How many goodly creatures are there here!
How beauteous mankind is! O brave new world
That has such people in't!

Shakespeare, *The Tempest*

•

"How you doing, honey?" he asks me that morning.
   "I feel like a million bucks!"
   "Don't worry." He laughs. "This, too, shall pass."
   "But I feel great."
   "Oh, Jesus." Bert shakes his head. "You're on the pink cloud."
   It's a temporary euphoria that follows the initial detox. He emphasizes the temporary part.

Domenica Ruta, *With or Without You*

•

You're on a pleasant cloud. . . . But then this good feeling leaves you. You realize where you are, and what you're doing there, and what has just happened to you. And what follows is a hurt, a confused hurt — not a physical hurt — it's a hurt combined with anger; it's a what-will-people-think hurt.

Floyd Patterson, quoted in *King of the World*

•

... when he realized that the various Substances he didn't used to be able to go a day without absorbing hadn't even like *occurred* to him in almost a week, Gately hadn't felt so much grateful or joyful as just plain shocked. The idea that AA might actually somehow *work* unnerved him. He suspected some sort of trap. Some new sort of trap. At this stage he and the other Ennet residents who were still there and starting to snap to the fact that AA might work began to sit around together late at night going batshit together because it seemed to be impossible to figure out just *how* AA worked. It did, yes, tentatively seem maybe actually to be working, but Gately couldn't for the life of him figure out how just sitting on hemorrhoid-hostile folding chairs every night looking at nose-pores and listening to clichés could work. Nobody's ever been able to figure AA out, is another binding commonality. And the folks with serious time in AA are infuriating about questions starting with *How*. You ask the scary old guys How AA Works and they smile their chilly smiles and say Just Fine. It just works, is all; end of story. The newcomers who abandoned common sense and resolve to Hang In and keep coming and then find their cages all of a sudden open, mysteriously, after a while, share this sense of deep shock and possible trap; about newer Boston AAs with like six months clean you can see this look of glazed suspicion instead of beatific glee, an expression like that of bug-eyed natives confronted suddenly with a Zippo lighter. And so this unites them, nervously, this tentative assemblage of possible glimmers of something like hope, this grudging move toward maybe acknowledging that this unromantic, unhip, clichéd AA thing—so unlikely and unpromising, so much the inverse of what they'd come too much to love — might really be able to keep the lover's toothy maw at bay. The process is the neat reverse of what brought you down and In here: Substances start out being so magically great, so much the interior jigsaw's missing piece, that at the start you just know, deep in your gut, that they'll never let you down; you just know it. But they do. And then this goofy slapdash anarchic system of low-rent gatherings and corny slogans and saccharin grins and hideous coffee is so lame you just *know* there's no way it could ever possibly work except for the utterest morons...and then Gately seems to find out AA turns out to be the very loyal friend he thought he'd had and then lost, when you Came In. And so you Hang In and stay sober and straight, and out of sheer hand-burned-on-hot-stove terror you heed the improbable-sounding warnings not to stop pounding out the nightly meetings even after the Substance-cravings have left and you feel like you've got a grip on the thing at last and can now go it alone, you still don't try to go it alone, you heed the improbable warnings because by now you have no faith in your own sense of what's really improbable and what isn't, since AA seems, improbably enough, to be working, and with no faith in your own senses you're confused, flummoxed, and when people with AA time strongly advise you to keep coming you nod robotically and keep coming...

David Foster Wallace, *Infinite Jest*

•

At the end of every meeting, all the alcoholics stand up and pray together. Holding hands, we break into a weird psychological cheer — "It works if you work it, and *you're worth it!*" I feel both my hands being squeezed by the strangers on either side of me. Such explicit self-confidence is embarrassing to me. But, then again, before all this I was ready to have some idiot's baby or throw myself in front of a train. So who am I to judge?

Domenica Ruta, *With or Without You*

•

It says in the program if you don't believe, pretend that you do. Fake it till you make it, they say. And I know that a lot of people have problems with that, but I follow the program. So I get down on my knees in the morning and say, God help me to not think of drink and drugs. And I get down on my knees at night and say, Thank you that I didn't have to drink or use.

Stephen King, interview, *Paris Review*

•

The God thing . . . If you read the literature, it doesn't matter what you believe in — you can believe in a horse or a tree — but it's so clearly about believing in God.

Lennard Davis, quoted in *Clean*

•

You ask me how to pray to someone who is not.
All I know is that prayer constructs a velvet bridge
And walking it we are aloft, as on a springboard,
Above landscapes the color of ripe gold
Transformed by a magic stopping of the sun.
That bridge leads to the shore of Reversal
Where everything is just the opposite and the word 'is'

Unveils a meaning we hardly envisioned.
Notice: I say we; there, every one, separately,
Feels compassion for others entangled in the flesh
And knows that if there is no other shore
We will walk that aerial bridge all the same.

Czeslaw Milosz, "On Prayer"

·

And almost every one when age,
    Disease, or sorrows strike him,
Inclines to think there is a God,
    Or something very like Him.

Arthur Hugh Clough, *Dipsychus*

6

·

When he kneels at other times and prays or meditates or
tries to achieve a Big-Picture spiritual understanding of
God as he can understand Him, he feels Nothing — not
nothing, but *Nothing*, an edgeless blankness that somehow feels worse than the sort of unconsidered atheism he
Came In with.

David Foster Wallace, *Infinite Jest*

·

You know who my gods are, who I believe in fervently?
Herman Melville, Emily Dickinson — she's probably the
top — Mozart, Shakespeare, Keats. These are wonderful
gods who have gotten me through the narrow straits of life.

Maurice Sendak, interview, *Fresh Air*

•

In many ways, Alcoholics Anonymous is a religious program—although this statement would no doubt provoke howls of protest from most group members.

Susan Cheever, *My Name Is Bill*

•

In truth, Serenus, I have for a long time been silently asking myself to what I should liken such a condition of mind, and I can find nothing that so closely approaches it as the state of those who, after being released from a long and serious illness, are sometimes touched with fits of fever and slight disorders, and, freed from the last traces of them, are nevertheless disquieted with mistrust, and, though now quite well, stretch out their wrist to a physician and complain unjustly of any trace of heat in their body. It is not, Serenus, that these are not quite well in body, but that they are not quite used to being well; just as even a tranquil sea will show some ripple, particularly when it has just subsided after a storm. What you need, therefore, is not any of those harsher measures which we have already left behind, the necessity of opposing yourself at this point, of being angry with yourself at that, of sternly urging yourself on at another, but that which comes last—confidence in yourself and the belief that you are on the right path, and have not been led astray by the many cross-tracks of those who are roaming in every direction, some of whom are wandering very near the path itself. But what you desire is something great and supreme and very near to being a god—to be unshaken.

Seneca, *Moral Essays*

•

What I've learned from my sobriety, from the men and women who keep me sober, is how to pray. Blind drunks who get sober get a kind of blind faith—not so much a vision of who God is, but who God isn't, namely me.

Thomas Lynch, "The Way We Are"

•

... I don't go to the meetings, so I've never worked my way through the twelve steps, like you're supposed to. It's not the God thing that puts me off, because you don't have to believe in God to do the program. You just have to accept that there's a higher power—it could be the lamp in the corner of the room, for all they care.

Ozzy Osbourne, *I Am Ozzy*

•

For a lot of folks who get sober, the process of getting and staying sober becomes their higher power, and it becomes a religion that sort of consumes a whole lot of them. I just don't think that that's necessary. I think that that can be a side note rather than the story of your life. I think a lot of people are scared, and I know I was scared to get sober, at least using this as an excuse; "I don't want to be one of those sober people." And I don't think you have to be. I think you can be one of those people who happens to be sober. For me, no, I'm not a particularly religious person. I was determined not to convert during that process.

Jason Isbell, interview, *Fresh Air*

•

One day, I decided to attend a support group for the children of alcoholics. It scared me speechless. The other people in the group were hard drinkers, which I was not. They got up in the morning and thought about alcohol, which I did not. They'd ruined marriages and lost jobs and wrecked automobiles because of alcohol, which I had not. All the same, I liked a drink or two when I came home from work. Sometimes more than two. Did this mean I was doomed to end up like them?

One night Francesca announced that she was pregnant for the second time. We soon found out that she was carrying a boy. My drinking days were over. It would be nice to think that I made a solemn vow to never put my son through what I'd been through as a child; but why then had I not stopped drinking when my daughter was born, two years earlier? No, it was more a case of fatigue with alcohol as a substance, a rationalization, a topic, a word. For thirty-five years, alcohol had been at the center of every conversation my family engaged in, and now I wanted that conversation to end. I didn't want to drink alcohol, think about alcohol, talk about alcohol. I wanted alcohol—as a beverage, a theme, a backdrop, a depressant, a leitmotif, an excuse, a casus belli—out of my life forever. I stopped drinking the day I found out that my wife was carrying a boy. I never drank again.

Joe Queenan, *Closing Time*

•

However many people AA helps, the fact is that it doesn't work for many, and there is a dire need for alternatives.

David Sheff, *Clean*

•

Many people in AA will do everything *but* break their anonymity outright, identifying themselves only as a "recovering alcoholic" or even as being "in a twelve-step program." I am still one of those hedgers, trying to write about recovery without violating the tradition—and all the while wondering if that's like pretending to be a little bit pregnant.

Susan Cheever, "Is it Time to Take the Anonymous out of AA?"

6

•

It seems crazy that we can't just be out with it, in this day and age. I don't want to have to hide my sobriety; it's the best thing about me.

Molly Jong-Fast, quoted in the *New York Times*

•

While a few things change, much remains the same. I used to be a miserable, spiritless, insecure egomaniac who smelled like whiskey. Now I am a well-intentioned, sometimes volatile, even more insecure egomaniac who smells like coffee. My friends in the recovery movement tell me that's just fine for now.

"Progress, not perfection," they say.

"You know, I really hate all the sententious crap you people spew out," I answer. "It makes me feel like a member of a brainless cult."

"That's okay, honey. You just keep coming."

Domenica Ruta, *With or Without You*

SEVEN

SHAKE-SPEARE'S CHILD

Family and Friends

I remember once, it was just before my birthday and I knew that Pappy was getting ready to start on one of these bouts. I went to him—the only time I ever did—and said, "Please don't start drinking." And he was already well on his way, and he turned to me and said, "You know, no one remembers Shakespeare's child." I never asked him again.

Jill Faulkner Summers

They give us the strength to live our lives; more, they give us life itself. They are the runway that we race along, furiously flapping, until we are suddenly airborne, only then thinking to look back, with gratitude and regret, as they dwindle below our feet.

Unless they don't dwindle. Unless they try to pull back the gift they gave. Unless they're hanging from our ankles, keeping us earthbound, watching everybody else soar away, the wound that won't heal, the injury we have to nurse forever because in its infliction we were also denied the ability to make it better.

Usually it's some blend of both, of lift and burden, help and hurt, a hall of mirrors, of passages and obstacles, comfort and contradiction. Family is eternity and today, a century ago and tomorrow. It is the fresh faces of our grandparents, gazing out at us from sepia, scallop-edged photographs. Our parents as newlyweds, his hair slicked back, her lipstick bright red, then, a few snapshots later, holding a tiny bundle of us, we the vessels, we the current model, whether baby birds who flee the nest at a touch or marionettes who linger, dangling, wondering whether we ever dare cut our strings.

Family is permanence that keeps changing. Before we have figured out our parents we are often parents ourselves, a new generation for us to look at with breathless wonder, while they return our stare, in mutual puzzlement and fascination, bound by a knot of infinite complexity, tangled together in an intricate way that blesses and damns, loves and hates, remembers and forgets.

As if this weren't complicated enough, there is not only your unique family but how you react to it as well. You can have the best family in the world—loving, generous, fun—yet it can make this struggle somehow worse. You resent them for being so nice. Or you could have some monster family, who hurt you at every turn and you still run to them, arms wide, awash in love, surprised every time.

Whatever the case, no clan is too tight or too loose, too loving or too cold, to be visited by the woes of addiction.

Nowhere can the damage of drinking or drugs be more clearly seen—if you can bear to look—than in the impact on your loved ones: your parents, children, spouses, relatives, friends. They have been there from the start, and the same pernicious monster that altered you has also altered them, as witnesses, bystanders, victims, dupes, co-conspirators, inspirations, or some tortured combination.

They will probably play an important role in the process you're going through. Rare is the solitary person who sheds addiction without having caught the attention of others; rarer still is the person who becomes sober alone, unprompted and unassisted by outside influence. Indeed, typically it is our loved ones who tell us first, long before we are willing to hear what they say, our family whose faces mirror our addictions so starkly that our initial impulse is to turn away.

Thus isolation becomes a central quality of substance abuse. You hide how much you drink. You go off by yourself to take your drugs. It isn't something you advertise. No one says, "I'll be right back mom—I'm going to guzzle some vodka in the bathroom."

Now, as you build your new life, you return to find the family and friends right where you left them. In AA, the eighth step is to make a list of all the persons you've harmed, and the ninth step is to apologize to them, provided that doing so won't hurt them further.

Who you apologize to or don't apologize to—or whose apology you accept or reject—is your business. While words can help you on your road to sobriety, this journey also underscores the limits of language. The most eloquent apology is to live your life without having to drink or take drugs all the time. You don't even have to tell anyone—they'll figure it out for themselves. Just as your problem probably wasn't the big secret you thought it was, so your recovery won't be secret either.

Your family will know. They will see you taking the hard way, making the right choices. And family can be a powerful motivation. Even if you aren't doing this for yourself, you can start by doing it for your loved ones, your children, your spouse. How has it affected them to have a drunk dad, a drug-abusing wife? How much better would their lives be if you could stay on the road to recovery? Getting sober for your family's benefit isn't the ideal reason, but it's enough, for starters, and you'll figure out later, when your judgment is no longer skewed, that you have been doing this for yourself, too.

Benefits will come, though probably not immediately, because your loved ones may be dubious—and rightly so. Remember: most recovering addicts climb up and slip back and must try again and again until they get it right. That isn't pretty to watch and inspires skepticism. You've said you've changed before but you didn't change. You promised to be different but you were the same. Now you're saying that you've changed. Again. That you are well intentioned and sincere might take the edge off the lie, should it turn out to be another lie, but it won't take the edge off their disappointment. The only persuasive argument now is to make recovery stick and wait until your loved ones see that it's real.

You can't demand trust—someone has to give it willingly. It has to be earned. In Al-Anon your family is taught to disengage from you. To step back from your self-absorbed drama and constant crisis, to let the only person who can figure it out and make it work—you—figure it out and make it work. Doing so will draw the people in your life back, gradually. Remember the value of time.

And remember the difference between trust and love. Love

isn't earned like trust; it's given, even to the undeserving. "Home is the place where, when you have to go there, they have to take you in," Robert Frost writes. But love can be abused away, can freeze up and become dormant. Living your life right will begin the slow thaw.

•

The whiskey on your breath
Could make a small boy dizzy;
But I hung on like death:
Such waltzing was not easy.

We romped until the pans
Slid from the kitchen shelf;
My mother's countenance
Could not unfrown itself.

The hand that held my wrist
Was battered on one knuckle;
At every step you missed
My right ear scraped a buckle.

You beat time on my head
With a palm caked hard by dirt,
Then waltzed me off to bed
Still clinging to your shirt.

Theodore Roethke, "My Papa's Waltz"

7

•

I never suspected a thing. Nor did my brother. We never saw any drug paraphernalia. There was a mysterious purplish spot in the crook of my father's elbow, which he said had something to do with the army. His vague explanation was unsatisfactory, but even in my wildest imaginings I never came near the truth. In the fifties, in the white, middle- and working-class communities where we lived, no one discussed drugs, which were synonymous with the utmost degradation and depravity. My parents succeeded in hiding my father's addiction from us, but, as a result, we could never make sense of the strained atmosphere, our lack of money, our many moves. The addiction was the thread that tied everything together. We didn't know that such a thread existed, and so decisions seemed insanely arbitrary.

Susan J. Miller, "Never Let Me Down"

•

I spent a lot of time in saloons as a boy. My father would sometimes treat me and my older sister to a movie, covering our eyes with his hands during the risqué sequences, then stop off at a nearby taproom for a few belts. We were usually not allowed to sit at the bar, as this sort of thing didn't sit well with bartenders or even with some of the patrons. Instead, he would plant us in the plush leather booths that ringed these establishments and bring us one ginger ale after another while he slowly got soused. When we were quite young, we thought such excursions a lark, because we could plunge our fingers down into the upholstery and excavate loose change that had tumbled out of someone's pockets and into these crevices. But as we grew older it was much less diverting to sit there for hours on end, watching our father slowly transform himself from a well-spoken gentleman into a brute spoiling for a fight. It was also less fun because nobody—not even a kid—wants to sit for three hours straight drinking thirteen glasses of ginger ale.

Joe Queenan, *Closing Time*

•

On afternoons when he came home from work sober, we flung ourselves at him for hugs, and felt against our ribs the telltale lump in his coat. In the barn we tumbled on the hay and heard beneath our sneakers the crunch of buried glass. We tugged open a drawer in his workbench, looking for screwdrivers or crescent wrenches, and spied a gleaming six-pack among the tools. Playing tag, we darted around the house just in time to see him sway on the rear stoop and heave a finished bottle into the woods.

Scott Russell Sanders, "Under the Influence"

•

SEYMOUR: What do you guys want to do?

ZACH: Let's find your dad's liquor and drink it!

SEYMOUR: Cool! The only thing is: I don't know where the old man keeps his booze.

DAN: Well, let's split up and look for it! There are *six* of us. One of us is bound to find it.

SEYMOUR: Awesome, let's do it!

(*Five minutes later.*)

ZACH: I found it! It was in the first place I looked!

DAN: Really? I found some too.

MIKE: Me too. Look.

KEVIN: I . . . I also found some alcohol.

7

SEYMOUR: Everyone found alcohol? I don't understand. Where did you guys look?

ZACH: Under your dad's bed.

DAN: In your dad's medicine cabinet.

JOSH: Behind your dad's toilet.

KEVIN: A few different closets. And in your little sister's room ... behind her community service trophies.

JAKE: I found a moonshine still in the basement. It looked pretty advanced. There were bags of barley and pressurized tanks. And there was some kind of silver tasting cup, hanging from a hook.

SEYMOUR: I can't believe this. I think I have to be alone for a while.

BRENT: (*running in*) Hey, Seymour! Guys! Guess what, I found the booze! You'll never guess where it was—in the attic inside an old box marked "Memories."

SEYMOUR: ...

BRENT: There was a lot up there.

Simon Rich, "Slumber Party"

•

Mother is drinking to forget a man
Who could fill the woods with invitations:
Come with me he whispered and she went
In his Nash Rambler, its dash
Where her knees turned green
In the radium dials of the '50s.

When I drink it is always 1953,
Bacon wilting in the pan on Cook Street
And mother, wrist deep in red water.
Laying a trail from the sink
To a glass of gin and back.
She is a beautiful, unlucky woman
In love with a man of lechery so solid
You could build a table on it
And when you did the blues would come to visit.
I remember all of us awkwardly at dinner.
The dark slung across the porch,
And then mother's dress falling to the floor,
Buttons ticking like seeds spit on a plate.
When I drink I am too much like her—
The knife in one hand and in the other
The trout with a belly white as my wrist.
I have loved you all my life
She told him and it was true
In the same way that all her life
She drank, dedicated to the act itself,
She stood at this stove
And with the care of the very drunk
Handed him the plate.

Lynn Emanuel, "Frying Trout while Drunk"

·

Drinking to handle the angst of Mother's drinking—
caused by her own angst—means our twin dipsomanias
face off like a pair of mirrors, one generation offloading
misery to the other through dwindling generations, back
through history to when humans first fermented grapes.

Mary Karr, Lit

•

The mice's preference was compelling because it clearly had nothing to do with upbringing, culture, peer pressure, stress, expectations, advertising, emotional trauma, or any other variable that can influence human drinking. The preference shown by the C57BL/Crgl mice was *internally* generated. They inherently liked the taste, the intoxication, or some other quality of the alcohol. Subsequent breeding bore this out. When alcohol-preferring mice were bred together, the inborn predilection strengthened: the grandchildren of the original mice drank more and drank higher concentrations of alcohol than their grandparents. Likewise, when mice that avoided alcohol were bred, their progeny became *less* willing to take even a sip of the hard stuff.

Stephen Braun, *Buzz*

•

My father was not a glamorous drunk. Sober he could enchant, charm, bewitch, con; Duke was a stutterer with a gift of gab. Drunk he was a stumblebum. Late at night as a kid, I'd hear the front door open, listen for the step. If his step was deliberate, we were in for it. After my mother had enough, and then my stepmother, I was in for it. We lived many places low and some high, but when he was high, high was worse. The stairs: he'd pull himself up a step at a time, muttering. There'd be a failure midway: he'd knock a picture off the wall, or lean too hard against the rail and break a baluster, or trip. Then he'd be on my bed reminding me what a miserable pismire I was, how I'd failed him, betrayed him, held him back, kicked him in the ass: *Old Lyme . . . Sarasota . . . Seattle . . . New York . . . Wilton . . . La*

Jolla: Screwed again. Then he'd be on his knees, driving the porcelain bus, heaving up his Dutch courage; then, next morning, he'd be on his knees, begging forgiveness for words he claimed he couldn't recall, words he maybe couldn't recall. I could recall them pitch-perfect, and what I wondered then: Is *veritas* in *vino*? If so, the truth had been said last night: I was a miserable pismire; he'd been sapped by me. Come morning, my dad wasn't interested in my metaphysical inquiry, but in his: "Why do I do it?" he'd ask me.

Maybe he liked it. Maybe he had a disease. Who cares? I'm sorry: *now* who cares? What I care to ask is why—knowing what I knew—did I do it? I could say genetics. I could read my journals and hear his melodramatic keening and explain: DNA dunnit. Raising a glass black with Wild Turkey, I'd cry cheers, to your health, bottoms up... just like Dad. Like him, I'd drink myself sick and call it a toot. I'd be *overtaken*, or say, like Duke, "It got drunk out last night and a little fell on me."

Geoffrey Wolff, *A Day at the Beach*

•

Billy's ROTC uniform was the source of his greatest pride as a young teenager. Perhaps because of that pride, the suit also later became for him an enduring symbol of disillusionment.

After joining the ROTC...Billy headed for Mountain Park, where his father still lived. He arrived at the old homestead to find Pop drunk and naked, wallowing in a bathtub filled with homemade beer. "There he was," Bill recalled with laughter decades later, "pissing in the beer and then scooping some out for a drink."

Todd DePastino, *Bill Mauldin*

•

It is difficult to feel sympathy for these people. It is difficult to regard some bawdy drunk and see them as sick and powerless. It is difficult to suffer the selfishness of a drug addict who will lie to you and steal from you and forgive them and offer them help. Can there be any other disease that renders its victims so unappealing?

Russell Brand, "My Life without Drugs"

•

The last I see [my father] he's blind in the cedars from drinking and every time I see him put the bottle to his mouth he don't suck out of it, it sucks out of him until he's shrunk so wrinkled and yellow even the dogs don't know him.

Ken Kesey, *One Flew over the Cuckoo's Nest*

•

you are the loch ness monster
it's been so long since you surfaced
no one believes you exist anymore

you are a submarine that has lost its power
you watch television through a periscope
you are a permanent bathrobe
you are a cow poking her head through a barbed wire fence
you are a gambler an hour after squandering the rent

you are going over niagara falls in a giant pill bottle
you have a bruised throttle
you are a road trip that's gone awry
you are a bird that stands on a railing
rubbing your wings together
then you climb back down
and you call that a try

Jeffrey McDaniel, "Zugzwang"

7

•

The handwriting on the wall was brutal but clear. Her husband was a lush. He had a bad temper, one he could no longer keep wholly under control now that he was drinking so heavily and his writing was going so badly. Accidentally or not accidentally, he had broken Danny's arm. He was going to lose his job, if not this year then the year after. Already she had noticed the sympathetic looks from the other faculty wives. She told herself that she had stuck with the messy job of her marriage for as long as she could. Now she would have to leave it.

Stephen King, *The Shining*

•

The house rocked and shouted all night.
Toward morning, grew quiet. The children,
looking for something to eat, make
their way through the crazy living room
in order to get to the crazy kitchen.
There's Father, asleep on the couch.
Sure they stop to look. Who wouldn't?

Raymond Carver, "From the East, Light"

•

It takes so little, so infinitely little, for a person to cross the border beyond which everything loses meaning: love, convictions, faith, history. Human life — and herein lies its secret — takes place in the immediate proximity of that border, even in direct contact with it; it is not miles away, but a fraction of an inch.

Milan Kundera, *The Book of Laughter and Forgetting*

•

If someone says: "I'm just going out to get cigarettes. I'll be back in 15 minutes" and you spend three days fielding telephone calls from his wife, you know there is something wrong.

Ivan Chermayeff, quoted in the *New York Times*

•

Nothing was ever said between us about drink. A man's family did not discuss this, or admit it.

Adela Rogers St. Johns, *Final Verdict*

•

I didn't want to hear *any* of what my family was telling me. My makeup wasn't smeared, I wasn't disheveled, I behaved politely, and I never finished off a bottle, so how could I be alcoholic?

Betty Ford, *Betty*

•

"Did you say Sebastian was drunk?"

"Yes."

"Extraordinary time to choose. Couldn't you stop him?"

"No."

"No," said Brideshead, "I don't suppose you could. I once saw my father drunk, in this room. I wasn't more than about ten at the time. You can't stop people if they want to get drunk. My mother couldn't stop my father, you know."

Evelyn Waugh, *Brideshead Revisited*

7

•

wants my son
wants my niece
wants josie's daughter
holds them hard
and close as slavery
what will it cost
to keep our children
what will it cost
to buy them back.

Lucille Clifton, "white lady (a street name for cocaine)"

•

I was no longer invited on family vacations, and my parents didn't try to come up with a plausible reason why: We just don't want to be with you, they would tell me. And I didn't even care. (Indeed, this past year, I was surprised to be told about a trip to Alaska my parents and siblings had taken while I was still using.) Whenever anyone in my family went out of town, they had to check in at least once a day in case I died. This wasn't maudlin, just the reality I had imposed on my family's lives.

Seth Mnookin, "Harvard and Heroin"

•

Maybe we shouldn't leave,
I say to my husband. I want
to want to go away—four-poster bed,
morning walks by the ocean
in fog so thick you have to trust
the rocky path continues, sweating
its many shades of gray. But I need
to give my son an article
I cut out of last Sunday's *Times,*
a perfect mantra for staying sober.
If we leave, I say, *something terrible*
may happen. My husband pours his coffee
down the sink, gets a new cup—
Something terrible is happening.
I pencil hard on the inn's brochure,
leaded lines crosshatching
the four-poster bed, the ruffled comforter.

Wendy Mnookin, "Relapse"

•

MARY

[*Her eyes become fixed on the whiskey glass on the table beside him—sharply.*]

Why is that glass there? Did you take a drink? Oh, how can you be such a fool? Don't you know it's the worst thing?

[*She turns on Tyrone.*]

You're to blame, James. How could you let him? Do you want to kill him? Don't you remember my father? He wouldn't stop after he was stricken. He said doctors were fools! He thought, like you, that whiskey is a good tonic!

[*A look of terror comes into her eyes and she stammers.*]

But, of course, there's no comparison at all. I don't know why I—Forgive me for scolding you, James. One small drink won't hurt Edmund. It might be good for him, if it gives him an appetite.

Eugene O'Neill, Long Day's Journey into Night

•

The predicament I found myself in was clear. My dad was a drunk, his dad was a drunk, his dad had probably been a drunk, and unless I played my cards right, I was going to end up a drunk, too. This was not shaping up as an idyllic childhood. The same held true for my sisters. We had landed in a perilous situation and our survival was by no means assured. We were going to need outside help, lots of it. I knew this to be a fact. I also knew that if I did not get a break, I was going to be crushed beneath the wheel like so many others who started out poor....If I did not get a break, I was going to end up exactly like my father, a miserable, deranged, booze-soaked failure.

Joe Queenan, Closing Time

•

I never knew him to lie about anything, ever, except about this one ruinous fact. Drowsy, clumsy, unable to fix a bicycle tire, throw a baseball, balance a grocery sack, or walk across the room, he was stripped of his true self by drink.

Scott Russell Sanders, "Under the Influence"

•

"It's no good Charles," she said. "All you can mean is that you have not as much influence or knowledge of him as I thought. It is no good either of us trying to believe him. I've known drunkards before. One of the most terrible things about them is their deceit. Love of truth is the first thing that goes."

Evelyn Waugh, *Brideshead Revisited*

•

To be an addict is to be something of a cognitive acrobat. You spread versions of yourself around, giving each person the truth he or she needs — you need, actually — to keep them at one remove.

David Carr, *The Night of the Gun*

•

Marge, it takes two to lie. One to lie and one to listen.

Matt Groening, *The Simpsons*

•

Friends and friends of friends offer contradictory advice: Kick him out, don't let him out of your sight. I think: Kick him out? What chance will he have then? Don't let him out of my sight? *You* try corralling a seventeen-year-old on drugs.

David Sheff, *Beautiful Boy*

•

"It ain't a question of his being a good boy," Mama said, "nor of his having good sense. It ain't only the bad ones, nor yet the dumb ones that gets sucked under."

James Baldwin, "Sonny's Blues"

•

7

My first resolve is to ask my family to help me with my drinking. Since I seem unable to handle it myself, I must find someone to help me. My second resolve, and this in a spate of bitterness, is that I will learn to disregard their interference. I think, abysmally bitter, that Orpheus knew he would be torn limb from limb; but he had not guessed that the Harpy would be his daughter. I lose at darts to my son and scold Mary about my dilemma. No money, no place to work in, no chair, even, to sit upon. I wake this morning, remorseful, exhausted, to begin a new year. The sky is the dark blue of high altitude.

John Cheever, journal entry, 1962

•

That day at McLean's, my mother sat down across from me in yet another well-meaning doctor's office in yet another institution. She adjusted her gray glasses, played with her hands and said: "This is it. Either you go to long-term treatment, or we are going to have to cut ourselves off. I will always love you," she said. "But I will not watch you kill yourself, and I will not let you do this to my family."

Seth Mnookin, "Harvard and Heroin"

•

DOROTHY: I'm frightened, Auntie Em! I'm frightened!

AUNTIE EM: [*image in crystal ball*] Dorothy? Dorothy? Where are you? It's me, Auntie Em. We're trying to find you. Where are you?

DOROTHY: I'm here in Oz, Auntie Em. I'm locked up in the Witch's castle, and I'm trying to get home to you, Auntie Em! Oh, don't go away.

> **Noel Langley, Florence Ryerson, and**
> **Edgar Allan Woolf,** *The Wizard of Oz*

•

My father called to me across the water;
Crouched in the little boat, I would not come,
But lingered on the blue and trembling waves,
Rowed in a circle, listening to the thrushes
Whistle themselves to sleep along the shore.
And so I slipped out of my father's hands
And moved as in a spell, across the lake
That shone like satin dipped in indigo.

Mist gathered then and hid me from the land.
I stowed the dripping oars, content to drift.
The evening stars flickered above my head
And burned like roses underneath the waves
As if I sailed above a second world, —
Till I forgot the earth of birds and leaves,
The shapes of trees, or how my happy town
Lay in the summer's vast and fragrant hills.

And so I traveled through the realms of night
And came to darkness like a witch's garden,
Where stars grew diamond hard and did not move
And under me a thickness fathoms deep
And black as pitch slid like a living thing—
Here is the place, I thought, where heroes come
To do their painful and mysterious deeds.
And then, once more, I heard my father call.
Blind in the dark, I let the long oars down
And cried out: Father, Father, I am lonely!
The stars are strange! Oh, come and fetch me home!

Somewhere a boat creaked on the shuffling lake;
Swiftly it cut across the heavy night,
Loomed up beside me, and my angry father
Swung through the dark and took the trailing oars.
The east grew pale, and light began to sweep
Over the lake where night still hung like vines,
And still I cried in terror to be saved.
And then, like bells across the distant hills,
Far off and faint, we heard the first birds singing.
My father turned,—the little boat was drifting;—
My father held me, and I fell asleep.

Mary Oliver, "The Lake"

•

Don't do anything but *wait*. Everything will pass, and
serenity and *accepted* mysteries and disillusionments, and
the tenderness of a few good people, and new opportunities and ever so much of life, in a word, will remain. You
will do all sorts of things yet, and I will help you. The only
thing is not to *melt* in the meanwhile.

Henry James, letter to Grace Norton, July 28, 1883

•

you were in your twenties, and I,
once hand on glass
and heart in mouth,
outdrank the Rahvs in the heat
of Greenwich Village, fainting at your feet—
too boiled and shy
and poker-faced to make a pass,
while the shrill verve
of your invective scorched the traditional South.

Now twelve years later, you turn your back.
Sleepless, you hold
your pillow to your hollows like a child;
your old-fashioned tirade—
loving, rapid, merciless—
breaks like the Atlantic Ocean on my head.

Robert Lowell, "Man and Wife"

•

by what logic
do you hoard
a single tendril
of something you want
dead?

If there is any presence among us
so powerful, should it not
multiply, in service
of the adored garden?

You should be asking
these questions yourself,
not leaving them
to your victims. You should know
that when you swagger among us
I hear two voices speaking,
one your spirit, one
the acts of your hands.

Louise Glück, "Clover"

•

I prayed ceaselessly for him, a desperate human prayer. Not for his life, no one could take that cup from him, but for the strength to endure the unendurable.

Patti Smith, *Just Kids*

•

Seth didn't want me to tell people about his drug use, and it was easy not to: I talked less and less with my friends. I felt I knew what they must be thinking: "He's still using drugs? Why don't you do something?" It was hard to show interest in my friends' concerns—a child cut from the lacrosse team, an overdue term paper. I avoided celebrations. I had no patience for the cheerful superficiality of cocktail banter, and I was jealous that other families had something to celebrate. Graduations and weddings left me gripping my wine glass, feeling selfish and maudlin, blinking back tears.

Wendy Mnookin, "My Son, the Junkie"

•

Her sister Marjorie, who knew all the secrets, finally decided that she must intervene in Elaine's life, and sometime around 1974 she taped one of Elaine's drunken discourses without her knowledge. Far from being amusing and witty, as Elaine fancied herself when she drank, she was rambling, incoherent and tiresome. Horrified, she vowed to quit drinking. It was her fear of losing control of the image she presented to the world that finally inspired her to seek treatment. She joined Alcoholics Anonymous, and with the help of three people—Marjorie, her therapist, and an Episcopalian priest—succeeded in breaking the addiction.

Mark Stevens and Annalyn Swan, *de Kooning*

•

SONYA: It's not like you! You're so elegant, you have that nice, soft voice. More than that even, more than anybody else I know, you're refined. Why would you want to be like ordinary people, drinking and gambling? Don't do it, I'm begging you. You always talk about how people don't create, they only destroy the beautiful things that they've been given. Why would you want to destroy yourself? Don't, don't please. I'm begging you, on my knees.

Anton Chekhov, *Uncle Vanya*

•

I threatened to leave if he didn't go to rehab. He finally said he'd do it, but making it happen and finding the right place was like pulling teeth. He insisted that it be someplace near the water, so we found a place near the water in Florida. The deal was he would stay there for thirty days and then I'd stay with him at Owl Farm.

He lasted a week. He had a drug dealer who lived in Florida bail him out of rehab and pick him up. That fucking guy called me and said he was going to pick Hunter up and take him to a plane, and I said, "Don't! Let him stay there." And he said, "Hey—it's *Hunter Thompson*, man..." That's when I realized that there would always be *that guy* who Hunter could get to go along with whatever he was doing. And there were more of them than there were of me.

Laila Nabulsi, quoted in *Gonzo*

•

He was an alcoholic. That was his real problem. It worked together with the drugs, of course, but with either one, you can't sustain the attention to structure, flow, and coherence that you need.

Jann Wenner, quoted in *Gonzo*

•

His wife tried to be gentle. "Remember how good your painting used to be when you weren't drinking?" she'd say, but her comments only reminded him of what he no longer was...Pollock's broken ankle was one more reminder of his rapidly deteriorating physical condition. With his bloated face, hazy features, and swollen, nicotine-stained fingers, he no longer was the commanding presence he had been only a year or two earlier.

Deborah Solomon, *Jackson Pollock*

•

In the turmoil of contradictory advice we received, the one consistent message came from Nar-Anon, the 12-step group for families of addicts. "Take care of yourselves," we were told. "Fix your own lives. The addict has to help himself."

This is not what we wanted to hear.

Wendy Mnookin, "My Son, the Junkie"

•

You're gonna have to save yourself this time darlin'
You're gonna have to find a soft heart in someone else
Cause I almost drowned comin' to your rescue
This time around, you're gonna have to save yourself

Beth Nielsen Chapman, "Save Yourself"

•

I can't save myself.
Somebody has got to save me,

I shall have to go through the world giving myself to
people until somebody will take me.

We are moving into a new studio at the front of the
wharf—
I am a little drunk—
the pain is dulled a little.

There is nothing.

Tennessee Williams, *Notebooks*, August 1940

•

According to Elaine Benson, who volunteered at the hospital, few people visited de Kooning in Southampton. And no one was there to pick him up. "I saw him sobering up maybe six times," she said. "He looked so small and Chaplinesque, with these hairless white legs hanging out of these hospital gowns. . . . You felt that nobody was taking care of him. He had this orphan quality." One time, Benson asked de Kooning when he was going to be released, and he said, "I think today, but I don't know if anybody is coming to get me."

Mark Stevens and Annalyn Swan, *de Kooning*

7

•

I remember getting a call very late one night from a bartender I happened to know at the White Horse Tavern telling me that there was "someone" over there "who says his name is Jack Kerouac," and who was totally smashed, but who also claimed he was sleeping at my place and would I come and pick him up? It was Jack, of course. Half a swallow away from complete collapse, and utterly alone. It seemed a damn shame. Though I never got through to him well enough to solve it. And then a few years later he was dead.

David Markson, "A Conversation with David Markson"

•

My wife's younger brother took heroin and died
in the bed he slept in as a boy across
the hall from the one she slept in as a girl.

He sold the pot he grew in their basement.
She'd leave work to take him to the clinic
but she understood she had to save herself.

No one saves themselves. Before I met my wife
I'd put on anything clean. My life dragged behind,
like a heavy shadow. I was resigned to anonymity.
I wanted to sleep. She gave my pain a bride.

Two months after he died, we hold hands
across a black sea, trying not to despise
the drunk at the next table, who doesn't
even try not to listen. It's best not to think
about the pain. To shut your eyes and float.

Our kids were jumping on our bed, windmilling,
in love with their capacity for delight.
When she answered the phone she shut her eyes.

He was a sweet young man who looked,
when we took him on his thirtieth birthday
to a restaurant filled with beautiful women,
as if he wanted to live forever.

When we visited his grave, the kids and I
wandered around in a city of the dead
and I could see her down the long avenues,
pulling weeds and staring at the ground.

At night she walks in the dark downstairs.
I know what she wants, to go to him the way
she goes to our boys when they're frightened,
to place herself between him and the pain.

Philip Schultz, "My Wife"

•

I longed for someone to scrape out every remnant of Nic
from my brain and scrape out the knowledge of what was
lost and scrape out the worry and not only my anguish but
his and the burning inside like I might scrape out the seeds
and juicy pulp of an overripe melon, leaving no trace of the
rotted flesh.

It felt as if nothing short of a lobotomy could alleviate
the unremitting pain.

David Sheff, *Beautiful Boy*

•

When I saw you outside the methadone clinic,
half your teeth gone, I had to turn, couldn't watch

the family tree being hacked into more firewood.
Yes, I want to crush and snort the knuckles

of the doctor who prescribed you the oblivion chiclets,
but you're the one playing Paul Bunyan, swinging

the pill bottle like a plastic ax, and my tongue
is not a ruby ambulance rushing toward you. I know

reality is a mosh pit that keeps spitting you out, that beauty
seeps from your face like sugar from a punctured sack.

I know death is on the staircase, but you were a ghost
all along, an apparition with a wineglass

floating through my childhood. I know you were born
in a Polish neighborhood with an aluminum spoon

in your mouth, that booze runs through us the way
politicians run through promises. I know the *more*

in morphine, what it's like to wake and feel like a chalk
outline of yourself. I know about days passing

so quickly they don't even wave, let alone stop
and say *hello*. I know it's been one of those months,

one of those lifetimes, when you dream of a laundromat,
a place to unscrew your skull and toss your dirty

thoughts in a machine, come back an hour later,
your impulses all folded and clean. If I could, I'd have a scientist

shrink me down and inject me into your bloodstream,
and I'll go with a wash brush and suds bucket,

scrub the opium out of each one of your cells. I used to think
I was tough because I could hold a machine gun

of whisky to my cranium and take bullet after bullet
to the brain. I used to think the greatest display of strength

was lifting a hunk of metal in the air, but now I know
it's far more difficult to put something down.

Jeffrey McDaniel, "Oblivion Chiclets"

•

In this country, don't forget, a habit is no damn private hell. There's no solitary confinement outside of jail. A habit is hell for those you love. And in this country it's the worst kind of hell for those who love you.

Billie Holiday, *Lady Sings the Blues*

•

7

Anyone who has lived through it, or those who are now living through it, knows that caring about an addict is as complex and fraught and debilitating as addiction itself. At my worst, I even resented Nic because an addict, at least when high, has a momentary respite from his suffering. There is no similar relief for parents or children or husbands or wives or others who love them.

David Sheff, *Beautiful Boy*

•

My wife, a former Al-Anon junkie who still goes to meetings whenever she's seriously stressed out, likes to tell people the standard line about the difference between the two groups. "Stand in the hall between two meetings and listen. From inside the A.A. room all you hear is laughter; from inside the Al-Anon room all you hear is tears."

Clancy Martin, "The Drunk's Club"

•

"Joey, I know I treated you and your sisters badly when you were kids," he began. "One of the things I've learned through Alcoholics Anonymous is that you have to admit that you've hurt people and let them know how sorry you are. I know that I did some bad things back then, and I apologize. Son, I'm sorry for anything I may have done to harm you."

Then he stuck out his hand.

I did not have it in me to forgive him, as absolution was not my line of trade, but I shook his hand anyway, if only because this creepy vignette made me uncomfortable and I wanted it to be over. Clemency was not included in my limited roster of emotions, but because he seemed to be making an effort to turn his life around, I did not express my true feelings at the time. Still, the whole thing rankled. I didn't like the way my father phrased his apology; it sounded like he was working from a script. I knew, of course, that the self-abnegation-by-numbers routine was a stunt suggested to people like my father by Alcoholics Anonymous. You had done many bad things and now realized that you were powerless before the fearsome suzerainty of demon alcohol, but you were man enough to fess up to your mistakes. You said a few words, you stuck out your hand—meekly, if you were any good at this sort of thing—your apology was accepted, and then everything was even-steven. . . . Nothing my father had done in all the years I'd known him infuriated me more than this fleabag apology.

Joe Queenan, *Closing Time*

•

One of the few upsides of my father being dead is that I can now break his anonymity and state plainly that he was a proud member of Alcoholics Anonymous for over 25 years. During that quarter-of-a-century span, he accumulated the most colorful, caring, fucked-up group of friends you'd ever want to see. It was a rag-tag band of misfits bound together only by their shared desire to not get loaded anymore. What a group. It was truly his greatest accomplishment. They all loved him in a way that even my brother and I had a hard time doing. He hadn't missed any of their birthdays or soccer games, and they saw only the man who had helped so many struggling folks get sober. They were by his side, uninterrupted, from diagnosis to death. Often annoying, but always a blessing, they gave him the greatest gift possible: their time. He was never alone. Not for one second.

Dax Shepard, "My Father's Horniness"

•

I cheated three of my children out of having a real father with them when they were young and I will always be sorry for that. I let them down when they were teenagers because of the example I set. I have little doubt that, in the case of Jeff and Laura, their own drug abuse was a twisted way for them to reach out and connect with me, get my attention, win my love and approval through emulation. It took a decade to turn my example around for them, but it has been, finally, well worth the struggle.

John Phillips, *Papa John*

•

The Redskins are winning
and I'm on the couch waiting for
the second half of their grunt-tussle
against the Chiefs to begin.

By ancient Indian habit,
I dash to the fridge for more suds.
For five years running now,
it's been this sad, non-alcohol beer
for me and my liver.
As usual, I read the health warning
before I drink the ersatz brew.
On the bottle's label, it says:

My brother, you are pouring
this illusion down your throat
because you are an alcoholic child
of alcoholic parents and they
were the alcoholic children
of your alcoholic grandparents.
My brother, oh, my brother
before your grandparents,
your great grandparents
lived without firewater,
without the ghost of electricity,
without the white man's God
in bow and arrow old-time days.
Days of obsidian. Days of grace.
Days of buckskin. Days of grace.
Days of the war lance and the buffalo.
Days before your people learned
how to hotwire
the Great Spirit
with chemical prayers.

Adrian C. Louis, "The Fine Printing on the
   Label of a Bottle of Non-Alcohol Beer"

•

But I should dishonor myself on this great occasion should I fail to declare to you that there is a monster evil in this beautiful land, born of the white man, that has swept away and destroyed many of our race; and now I here warn fathers and mothers, sons and daughters that, almost unseen, this deadly monster stalks abroad among us at noonday and at midnight. It is the serpent of the still. Pokagon hates this loathsome snake. There is no place so guarded or secluded in this land as not to be cursed by it. It crawls about your lawns and farms, along your highways and railways, drinks from your springs and wells, enters your homes, hides itself in the folds of your blankets, and crawls among your children while you sleep. . . . I urged upon you as you value the grand domain you inherit, as you value society, home and all that life holds most dear, to try and do all you can to banish this reptilian monster from your land; then heaven will smile upon you.

Chief Simon Pokagon, speech delivered August 16, 1894, in Angola, Indiana

•

I am grateful for his clear eyes and steady hands, his ability to work, his sense of humor. I can't say there are whole days when I don't worry, but there are hours.

I also grieve. I grieve for the years overwhelmed by his addiction, years when I was lost to my family, my writing, my self. I grieve for the loss of my optimism, the enthusiasm I used to feel that is now so hard to reclaim.

I grieve for the relationship I used to have with Seth, the relationship I might have had with him now, one of openness and trust. I do not know how long it will take to rebuild that intimacy, or if that is still possible.

I remember thinking when Seth was born that I would give my life to save his. Now I know that if he slips, there is nothing I can do.

Wendy Mnookin, "My Son, the Junkie"

•

When [my father] went into rehab, he was just this sour—he was ready to die. He just sat around criticizing all the time. You could just tell he was miserable. And so he made everybody else miserable. And he came out of rehab and started going to AA meetings, and he was a completely different person. He was totally engaged with the world. He suddenly wanted to learn how to work the dishwasher so that he could take care of himself . . . he was funny, he was empathetic, he was concerned. You know, he was involved in other people's lives. I mean, he had a change of heart that blew us all away.

Susan Cheever, interview, *On Being*

•

Our annual birthday do: dinner at
the Arizona Inn for only two.
White tablecloth, much cutlery, décor

in somber dark-beamed territorial style.
No wine, thank you. Determined to prolong
our second marriages, we gave that up,
with cigarettes. We toast each other's health
in water and a haze of candlelight.

My imitation of a proper man,
white-haired and wed to aging loveliness,
has fit me like a store-bought suit, not quite
my skin, but wearing well enough. . . .

John Updike, "Endpoint"

•

In August, 1988, my father was diagnosed with liver cancer, the result of chronic hepatitis, a disease associated with heroin addiction. The doctors correctly predicted he would live for five months. . . . My mother, who had stuck by him through everything, was still by his side. He was eager to share his latest revelation. A social worker in the treatment program had asked him what he would miss most when he died. It was an interesting question, and I was interested to hear his answer. He said: I told her that, yeah, sure, I'll miss my wife and my kids, but what I'll miss most is the music. The music is the only thing that's never let me down.

That the revelation would hurt us — my mother especially — never occurred to him. He never kept his thoughts to himself, even if it was cruel to express them. Neither my mother nor I said a word. The statement was the truth of him — not only what he said, but also the fact that he would say it to us, and say it without guilt, without apology, without regret.

Susan J. Miller, "Never Let Me Down"

7

•

That is how the story ends for my father, age sixty-four, heart bursting, body cooling and forsaken on the linoleum of my brother's trailer. The story continues for my brother, my sister, my mother, and me, and will continue so long as memory holds.

Scott Russell Sanders, "Under the Influence"

•

You are past love, praise, indifference, blame.

Thomas Hardy, "Your Last Drive"

•

I hold a five-year diary that my mother kept
for three years, telling all she does not say
of your alcoholic tendency. You overslept,
she writes. My God, father, each Christmas Day
with your blood, will I drink down your glass
of wine? The diary of your hurly-burly years
goes to my shelf to wait for my age to pass.
Only in this hoarded span will love persevere.
Whether you are pretty or not, I outlive you,
bend down my strange face to yours and forgive you.

Anne Sexton, "All My Pretty Ones"

•

People do what they can; they were good people,
They cared for us and loved us. Once they stood
Tall in my childhood as the school, the steeple.
How can I judge without ingratitude?

Judgment is simply trying to reject
A part of what we are because it hurts.
The living cannot call the dead collect:
They won't accept the charge, and it reverts.

It's my own judgment day that I draw near,
Descending in the past, without a clue,
Down to that central deadness: the despair
Older than any hope I ever knew.

James McAuley, "Because"

•

I wondered if that was how forgiveness budded, not with
the fanfare of epiphany, but with pain gathering its things,
packing up, and slipping away unannounced in the middle
of the night.

Khaled Hosseini, *The Kite Runner*

•

(In my sleep I dreamed this poem)

Someone I loved once gave me
a box full of darkness.

It took me years to understand
that this, too, was a gift.

Mary Oliver, "The Uses of Sorrow"

EIGHT

UPON BREACH OF MY LATE VOWS

Relapse

. . . and so to the pewterers to buy a poore's-box
to put my forfeits in, upon breach of my late vowes.

Samuel Pepys, diary entry, March 5, 1662

The vows that Samuel Pepys, the famously frank English diarist, had solemnly made to God a few days before, and would make time and time again, were to stop drinking wine and attending plays, two pleasures entwined in his mind. Putting aside the lure of the theater—then considered practically a mortal sin—Pepys offers ample evidence that long before there was the word "alcoholism," there was the snare of drinking and its damaging effects, the struggle to resist and the tendency of that resistance to eventually collapse.

Two and a half weeks after buying a slotted box to hold the coins he fined himself for submitting to wine, Pepys is back at it. "And so to supper and to bed," he writes, on March 22, 1662, after reveling with several ship owners, an alderman, and a captain, "having drank a great deal of wine."

The problem started early with Pepys, as it often does. Almost all that is known of Pepys's college years at Oxford is a written reprimand chiding him and a classmate for being caught "scandalously overserved with drink the night before."

The lure of the wine shop would dog him well beyond college. In his diary, which covers most of the 1660s, when he was in his late twenties and early thirties, he presents a detailed portrait of a busy bureaucrat—he was a high official in the English navy. Pepys (pronounced "peeps") was a prominent figure in Restoration London—acquainted with both Charles II and Isaac Newton—a man consumed with desires: to earn a lot of money, to grope every pretty maid or underling's wife who crossed his path, and to engage in a steady rondo of drinking then swearing off drinking. No detail was too trivial or too self-absorbed to escape Pepys's attention, and shame seldom caused him to halt his pen, creating not only an invaluable historical record but also a unique portrait of a man in the throes of addiction. If there were ever a writer who conveyed the maddening, tiresome, head-on-a-board repetition of relapse, it is Samuel Pepys.

Then and now, relapse is perhaps the thorniest problem in recovery. To acknowledge that it happens—that addicts routinely toss away their hard-fought-for sobriety—can sound to the desperate drunk trying to pick the lock on the cellar door like a kind of permission: I'm supposed to do this? It's *expected* of me? Thank merciful God.

But to ignore relapse invites the user to completely surrender after a single aborted attempt at sobriety, when usually it takes more than one, if not many tries. The mountain trail is steep and slippery. Few get it right the first time. And having gotten it right is no guarantee of future success, which is why people generally say they are "in recovery" and avoid claiming to have "recovered."

So the trick is to learn about relapse, then tuck the knowledge away and forget about it, like an insurance card in your wallet to be taken out in case of emergency. Hopefully you never use it. It's far easier if you don't have to. Then again "easy" is not a concept of much practical use in recovery.

Perhaps the clearest way to consider relapse is this: it's the risk that arises when the clamoring woes of addiction have been sufficiently muted by abstinence so that the siren call of an adored substance can be heard again. The court case has been dealt with. The family is happy and trusting. Time has rolled by. You've shaken off the horrible consequences, now safely relegated to the dimming past. Everything has returned to normal, to near normal. Yet something is missing.

Ironically, the better you get, the greater the risk of relapse can become, as your troubled times recede and become less immediate, more historical. You have to force yourself to remember that tempting though it may always be, using is still a danger, because along with the parts you loved come all the aspects that made you have to give it up.

Or as David Foster Wallace wrote in his epic novel, *Infinite Jest*—a significant part of which is a grotesque portrayal of addiction—while listing insights learned in rehab: "That nobody who's ever gotten sufficiently addictively enslaved by a Substance to need to quit the Substance and has successfully quit it for a while and been straight and but then has for whatever reason gone back and picked up the Substance again has *ever* reported being glad that they did it, used the Substance again and gotten re-enslaved; not ever."

That is a hard truth. Relapse is not so much eyes-open surrender to the delusion of addiction but, rather, a willful blindness, a too-complete return to who you used to be. The weeks turn into months, months into years, and suddenly that drinking problem can seem like a bad dream. Maybe it isn't true anymore. Maybe it was *never* true. And wouldn't that be something to celebrate? Or at least cut this boredom. Or make this painful feeling go away. Or because it's Christmas. Maybe one drink won't hurt . . . and if one doesn't, and sometimes it doesn't, or, rather, doesn't seem to at first, then the second might be okay, too, and off you go.

Relapse feels wonderful—initially. The lost child running into his mother's arms. The missing keys—there!—right where you left them. Odysseus, home at last, draws his bow. People don't relapse because it's awful, but because it's delightful, for a brief time.

Were relapse the end, but it's not the end. Nor is it the beginning again, but something far worse. Because this isn't the old love but the monster in disguise, no longer slain but returned to life, rousing at your tentative touch. Sooner or later—usually sooner—the problem reexerts itself, as the first slip becomes the second and the second the third and it comes time to stop, the moment when an unafflicted person would easily stop. But of course you can't stop because the problem was there all along, waiting.

You knew the trap was there and you walked right into it anyway. Clamped your eyes shut and hopped into the hole. Now you're stuck. Back to square one. Worse, because this is drinking or drug taking without illusions, the fulfilling of a need, as romantic as going to the bathroom. Yet, people return, often. Some people. Many, but not everybody. Relapse can be held at bay. Pepys seems nothing short of amazed when he manages to resist drinking.

"Thence to dinner, by Mr. Gaudens invitation," he records on June 12, 1662, "to the Dolphin, where a good dinner. But which is to myself a great wonder, that with ease I passed the whole dinner without drink[ing] a drop of wine. After dinner to the office, my head full of business, and so home."

Samuel Pepys eventually stopped drinking wine in taverns almost completely and lived to be seventy, an advanced age at the time.

•

To forget the world's abundance, even briefly and in a moment of spiritual penury, is to lose one's toehold on the ladder.

8

Robert M. Coates and E. B. White,
New Yorker, November 29, 1952

•

Those venal and furtive loves filled him with despair. He gnawed the rectitude of his life; he felt that he had been outcast from life's feast.

James Joyce, *"A Painful Case"*

•

But when he was cured and back in his senses he told them: "You think you've cured me but actually you've killed me. The illusion you took away was what I lived on."

Horace, *The Epistles of Horace*

•

Now that I am cured, I feel empty, poor, heartbroken and ill. The day after tomorrow I leave the clinic. Where should I go?

Jean Cocteau, *Opium*

•

Johnson observed, that the force of our early habits was so great, that though reason approved, nay, though our senses relished a different course, almost every man returned to them. I do not believe there is any observation upon human nature better founded than this; and in many cases, it is a very painful truth . . .

James Boswell, *The Life of Samuel Johnson*

•

The most common outcome of detoxification, by whatever means and for however long, is relapse.

Walter Ling, director of the Integrated
Substance Abuse Programs, UCLA

•

When you keep hearing "Relapse is part of recovery, relapse is part of recovery" each night from a different person, sometimes two or three, and then you leave the meeting and see the neon beer signs of the bar on the other side of Main, well, those lights get a little sparklier.

Clancy Martin, "The Drunk's Club"

•

After I had cut off my hands
and grown new ones

something my former hands had longed for
came and asked to be rocked.

After my plucked out eyes
had withered, and new ones grown

something my former eyes had wept for
came asking to be pitied.

8

    Denise Levertov, "Intrusion"

.

    the giant
    returns
    the giant
    retreats

    the giant
    returns
    the giant
    retreats

    the giant
    walks

    the giant
    sleeps

    the giant
    returns

    the giant
    retreats

Robert Lax, "[giant/returns]"

•

How came any reasonable being to subject himself to such a yoke of misery, voluntarily to incur a captivity so servile, and knowingly to fetter himself with such a seven-fold-chain?

Thomas De Quincey, *Confessions of an English Opium-Eater*

•

"I did that," says my memory. "I could not have done that," says my pride and remains inexorable. Eventually—the memory yields.

William Friedrich Nietzsche, *Beyond Good and Evil*

•

What then, you ask, is an evil? It is the yielding to those things which are called evils; it is the surrendering of one's liberty into their control, when really we ought to suffer all things in order to serve this liberty. Liberty is lost unless we despise those things which put the yoke upon our neck.

Seneca, Epistle 85

•

Waves of despair, waves of hopeless longing and heartache.
Waves of the mysterious wild hungers of youth, the dreams
    of childhood.
Detailed, urgent; once in a while, selfless.

All different, except of course
the wish to go back. Inevitably
last or first, repeated
over and over —

So the echo lingered. And the wish
held us and tormented us

Louise Glück, "Fable"

•

Like love, like seasickness, the craving penetrates everywhere. Resistance is useless. At first a malaise, then things
become worse. Imagine a silence equivalent to the crying
of thousands of children whose mothers do not return to
give them the breast. The lover's anxiety transposed into
nervous awareness. An absence which dominates, a nega-
tive despotism.

Jean Cocteau, *Opium*

•

You do look a little ill.
But we can do something about that, now.
Can't we.
The fact is you're a shocking wreck.
Do you hear me.
You aren't all alone.
And you could use some help today, packing in the
dark, boarding buses north, putting the seat back and
grinning with terror flowing over your legs through
your fingers and hair . . .

I was always waiting, always here.
Know anyone else who can say that.
My advice to you is think of her for what she is:
one more name cut in the scar of your tongue.
What was it you said, "To rather be harmed than
harm, is not abject."
Please.
Can we be leaving now.
We like bus trips, remember. Together
we could watch these winter fields slip past, and
never care again,
think of it.
I don't have to be anywhere.

Franz Wright, "Alcohol"

•

The beauty of quitting is, now that I've quit, I can have one, because I quit.

Jim Jarmusch, *Coffee and Cigarettes*

•

I AM DRINKING NOW... I am now drinking my pre-flight Bloody Mary to calm me. I feel protected by ½ of a Bloody Mary and the plane feels safe—an escape—another escape from the real world waiting for me.

Spalding Gray, *The Journals of Spalding Gray,*
September 3, 1991

•

Captain Cock and I had a breast of veale roasted. And here I drank wine upon necessity, being ill for want of it. And I find reason to fear that by my too sudden leaving off wine, I do contract many evils upon myself.

Samuel Pepys, diary entry, February 17, 1662

8

•

And the burnt Fool's bandaged finger goes wabbling back to the Fire.

Rudyard Kipling, "The Gods of the Copybook Headings"

•

The rat stops gnawing the wood, the dungeon walls withdraw, the weight is lifted. Nerve ends that stuck through your skin like bristles when you blotted the last line or shut the office door behind you have withdrawn into their sheaths. Your pulse steadies and the sun has found your heart.

Bernard DeVoto, *The Hour*

•

Addiction is when you do the thing you really, really most don't want to be doing.

Philip Seymour Hoffman, quoted in the *New York Times*

•

This was what always happened. I would be at pains to put my universe in order and set it ticking, when suddenly it would burst again into a mess of the same poor pieces.

Iris Murdoch, *Under the Net*

•

He told me I might now have the pleasure to see Dr. Johnson drink wine again, for he had lately returned to it. When I mentioned this to Johnson, he said, "I drink it now sometimes, but not socially." The first evening that I was with him at Thrale's, I observed he poured a large quantity of it into a glass, and swallowed it greedily. Every thing about his character and manners was forcible and violent; there never was any moderation; many a day did he fast, many a year did he refrain from wine; but when he did eat, it was voraciously, when he did drink wine, it was copiously. He could practice abstinence, but not temperance.

James Boswell, *The Life of Samuel Johnson*

•

I fell off my disciplined waggon last night with a thunderous crash and sat up with Brook until 5.30 in the a.m. drinking in the mean-time a whole bottle of Scotch alone.

Richard Burton, diary entry, September 29, 1969

•

...a wineglassful won't make a man drunk when he has already emptied a barrel.

> **Anton Chekhov,** letter to Madame M. V. Kiselyov,
> January 14, 1887

8

•

I'm on the wagon.... No hard liquor. Only beer.

> **F. Scott Fitzgerald,** *The Lost Summer*

•

And as soon as the morning's work was done, I was out of the house and away downtown to get my first drink. Merciful goodness!—if John Barleycorn could get such sway over me, a non-alcoholic, what must be the sufferings of the true alcoholic, battling against the organic demands of his chemistry while those closest to him sympathize little, understand less, and despise and deride him?

> **Jack London,** *John Barleycorn*

•

The quaking of the solid ground underfoot, the dropping-out of the bottom of things.

> **Thomas Mann,** "Early Sorrow"

•

The guests tried to make sense of the ugly events they had witnessed. Perhaps it had something to do with the cold weather—had he poured the drink simply because he was cold?—or perhaps with the movie, or perhaps with the death of Dr. Heller seven months earlier. No explanation seemed adequate as they considered the fact that the past two years of Pollock's life, sober years, had been his most rewarding ever.

Deborah Solomon, *Jackson Pollock*

•

And thus the whirligig of time brings in his revenges.

William Shakespeare, *Twelfth Night*

•

The next day he is up in time to help with the chores. He is deathly pale and his hands shake. Nobody mentions his absence and he is not apologetic—just withdrawn. As if he had answered a summons and is in no way responsible for what followed.

William Maxwell, *So Long, See You Tomorrow*

•

Not working is terribly painful and I'm still having a fight with the booze. I've enlisted the help of a doctor but it's touch and go. A day for me; a day for the hootch.

John Cheever, letter to William Maxwell, March 6, 1969

•

i was talking to a moth
the other evening
he was trying to break into
an electric light bulb
and fry himself on the wires

why do you fellows
pull this stunt i asked him
because it is the conventional
thing for moths or why
if that had been an uncovered
candle instead of an electric
light bulb you would
now be a small unsightly cinder
have you no sense

plenty of it he answered
but at times we get tired
of using it
we get bored with the routine
and crave beauty
and excitement
fire is beautiful
and we know that if we get
too close it will kill us
but what does that matter
it is better to be happy
for a moment
and be burned up with beauty
than to live a long time
and be bored all the while

so we wad all our life up
into one little roll
and then we shoot the roll
that is what life is for

it is better to be part of beauty
for one instant and then cease to
exist than to exist forever
and never be a part of beauty
our attitude toward life
is come easy go easy
we are like human beings
used to be before they became
too civilized to enjoy themselves

and before i could argue him
out of his philosophy
he went and immolated himself
on a patent cigar lighter
i do not agree with him
myself i would rather have
half the happiness and twice
the longevity

but at the same time i wish
there was something i wanted
as badly as he wanted to fry himself

Don Marquis, "the lesson of the moth"

•

His son Phelim told the story of Ronnie going back on "the gargle" as he periodically did. Feeling hung-over the following morning, he stopped on his way into town and went into a pub and ordered a gin and tonic. The pub was empty, but for a man at the far end sullenly looking into his first pint of the day. They drank in silence and then the voice from the other end of the bar said: "I thought you were off the drink."

"I am," replied Ronnie, "but I have a gin and tonic every now and again. I find it helps me to mind my own business. Would you like one?"

Ronnie Drew's obituary, *Independent*

•

Don't confront me with my failures. I had not forgotten them.

Jackson Browne, "These Days"

•

Yes, he knew that he was now withdrawing from everything: not merely from human beings. A moment more and everything will have lost its meaning, and that table and the cup, and the chair to which he clings, all the near and the commonplace, will have become unintelligible, strange and heavy... I say to myself: "Nothing has happened," and yet I was only able to understand that man because within me too something is happening, that is beginning to draw me away and separate me from everything.

Rainer Maria Rilke, *The Notebooks of Malte Laurids Brigge*

•

Having been so drunk yesterday felt terrible in morning and was desperately ill. Went quietly at 9.30 to find a double brandy. Bar closed until 10. Asked for Fritz (manager). Reluctantly he opened bar for me and suggested vodka as it wouldn't be so smelly when E had morning kiss. Drank it with very shaking hands. Have become a "falling down."

Richard Burton, diary entry, October 22, 1975

•

She had firm faith in...the principle that things done on the sly are not really done at all.

Evelyn Waugh, *Brideshead Revisited*

•

Morals first gave way as it were, then sank lower and lower, and finally began the downward plunge which has brought us to the present time, when we can endure neither our vices nor their cure.

Livy, *The History of Rome*

•

"Why are you drinking?" the little prince asked.

"To forget," replied the drunkard.

"To forget what?" inquired the little prince, who was already feeling sorry for him.

"To forget that I'm ashamed," confessed the drunkard, hanging his head.

"What are you ashamed of?" inquired the little prince, who wanted to help.

"Of drinking!" concluded the drunkard, withdrawing into silence for good. And the little prince went on his way, puzzled.

Antoine de Saint-Exupéry, *The Little Prince*

8

•

For the shoe pinches, even though it fits perfectly.

John Ashbery, "The Ecclesiast"

•

I have by a late oath obliged myself from wine and plays, of which I find good effect.

Samuel Pepys, diary entry, May 30, 1662

•

But how can one be happy who is still able, or rather who is still bound, to crave something else?

Seneca, Epistle 85

•

Drank a cup of ale and a toast, which I have not done many a month before, but it served me for my two glasses of wine to-day.

Samuel Pepys, diary entry, September 14, 1662

•

"We are lost, afflicted only this one way:
   That having no hope, we live in longing." I heard
   These words with heartfelt grief that seized on me

Knowing how many worthy souls endured
   Suspension in that Limbo. "Dear sir, my master,"
   I began, wanting to be reassured

In the faith that conquers every error, "Did ever
   Anyone go forth from here — by his own good
   Or perhaps another's — to join the blessed, after?"

Dante Alighieri, *Inferno*

•

Man is stupefied to see in his own case that the general rule
is shown to be true.

Giacomo Leopardi, *Zibaldone*

•

He who seeks to approach his own buried past must con-
duct himself like a man digging. Above all, he must not be
afraid to return again and again to the same matter; to scatter it as one scatters earth, to turn it over as one turns over
soil. For the "matter itself" is no more than the strata which
yield their long-sought secrets only to the most meticulous
investigation. That is to say, they held those images that,
severed from all earlier associations, reside as treasures in
the sober rooms of our later insights.

Walter Benjamin, "Excavation and Memory"

•

The truth is he with kindness did drink more than I believe he used to do, and did begin to be a little impertinent—the more when after all he would in the evening go forth with us and give us a bottle of wine abroad. And at the tavern met with an acquaintance of his that did occasion impertinent discourse, that though I honour the man, and he do declare abundance of learning and worth, yet I confess my opinion is much lessened of him. And therefore let it be a caution to myself not to love drink, since it has such an effect upon others of greater worth in my own esteem. I could not avoid drinking of five glasses this afternoon with him.

Samuel Pepys, diary entry, September 17, 1662

•

This day my oaths for drinking of wine and going to plays are out, and so I do resolve to take a liberty today, and then to fall to them again.

Samuel Pepys, diary entry, September 29, 1662

•

Strange to see how easily my mind do revert to its former practice of loving plays and wine, having given myself a liberty to them but these two days; but this night I have again bound myself to Christmas next, in which I desire God to bless me and preserve me, for under God I find it to be the best course that ever I could take to bring myself to mind my business.

Samuel Pepys, diary entry, September 30, 1662

•

He saw that all the struggles of life were incessant, laborious, painful, that nothing was done quickly, without labor, that it had to undergo a thousand fondlings, revisings, moldings, addings, removings, graftings, tearings, correctings, smoothings, rebuildings, reconsiderings, nailings, tackings, chippings, hammerings, hoistings, connectings — all the poor fumbling uncertain incompletions of human endeavor. They went on forever and were forever incomplete, far from perfect, refined, or smooth, full of terrible memories of failure and fears of failure, yet, in the way of things, somehow noble, complete, and shining in the end.

Jack Kerouac, *The Town and the City*

•

Let all such fancies, illusive and destructive, be banished henceforward from your thoughts forever. Resolve, and keep your resolution; choose, and pursue your choice. If you spend this day in study, you will find yourself still more able to study tomorrow; not that you are to expect that you shall at once obtain a complete victory. Depravity is not very easily overcome. Resolution will sometimes relax, and diligence will sometimes be interrupted; but let no accidental surprise or deviation, whether short or long, dispose you to despondency. Consider these failings as incident to all mankind. Begin again where you left off, and endeavor to avoid the seducements that prevailed over you before.

Samuel Johnson, quoted in *The Life of Samuel Johnson*

•

Of all the pitfalls in our paths and the tremendous delays
and wanderings off the track I want to say that they are not
what they seem to be. I want to say that all that seems like
fantastic mistakes are not mistakes, all that seems like error
is not error; and it all has to be done. That which seems like
a false step is the next step.

Agnes Martin, *Writings*

8

•

Left off the highway and
down the hill. At the
bottom, hang another left.
Keep bearing left. The road
will make a Y. Left again.
There's a creek on the left.
Keep going. Just before
the road ends, there'll be
another road. Take it
and no other. Otherwise,
your life will be ruined
forever. There's a log house
with a shake roof, on the left.
It's not that house. It's
the next house, just over
a rise. The house
where trees are laden with
fruit. Where phlox, forsythia,
and marigold grow. It's
the house where the woman

stands in the doorway
wearing sun in her hair. The one
who's been waiting
all this time.
The woman who loves you.
The one who can say,
"What's kept you?"

Raymond Carver, "Waiting"

•

Okay. Start over. It felt he would not be fighting withdrawal
this time, either. He'd find out what the *hell* was wrong and
fix it. Submit was the ticket. He was prepared with all his
power for anything.

John Berryman, *Recovery*

•

MARGE: I'm sorry Maggie, but growing up means giving
up the things you love.

Bill Odenkirk, *The Simpsons*

•

My second visit to Hazelden was, on the face of it, much
like the first, but, on a deeper level, it was very different.
This time I had no reservations about why I was there — I
had tried to control my drinking and failed — so there was
no more debate, no more gray area for me. Also, my life
had become very complicated and completely unmanageable during my relapse. I now had two children, neither of
whom I was really administering to; a broken marriage; as-

sorted bewildered girlfriends; and a career that, although it was still chugging along, had lost its direction. I was a mess.

Eric Clapton, *Clapton*

8

•

When I arrived at Silver Hill Hospital in New Canaan, Connecticut, I was a mess. I felt naked and fragile and hadn't touched my guitar since the embarrassing public performance a few weeks earlier. I'd convinced the admissions staff to allow me to keep an instrument in the room. They reluctantly agreed.

I now understand why they didn't want me to have access to my guitar. Suicide attempts are regular events in rehab, and guitar strings are perfect for hanging yourself. The staff at the hospital was sure that I, patient Nile Rodgers, was not ready to succeed in rehab, at least not this time around. They thought I was just too self-centered and too entrenched in my lifestyle to stop.

What the staff didn't know was that thanks to my bender on Madonna's thirty-sixth birthday, three days before I arrived at Silver Hill, I'd already stopped. I had had enough. The thing is, *stopping* wasn't hard at all. Every addict I know stops all the time — over and over and over again. And I, like every good addict, had stopping down cold. Stopping was easy; staying stopped was the hard part.

So I refocused on *staying* stopped, which, paradoxically, meant doing something instead of doing nothing. Hmm . . . this made sense to me. Anything of value (even drugs) that I had ever achieved required action and discipline. Double hmm . . . I remembered one of my teacher's words at the end of a lesson: "The only thing to remember is this simple definition of the word 'discipline': *the ability to delay gratification.* It's an easy way to visualize the training required to adopt a behavioral pattern."

Nile Rodgers, *Le Freak*

•

The last of man's great unchained beasts
lies lappin' at my door
The last of man's great unchained beasts
lies lapping at my door
And I'd be happy to give it what it wants
But I do know, it would just ask for more

Michael Timmins, "Mariner's Song"

•

The path up there is so steep that it is a conquest every time you climb it.

Albert Camus, *Notebooks*, 1936

•

But, however, as soon as I came home I did pay my Crowne to the poor's box, according to my vowe, and so no harm as to that is done, but only business lost and money lost, and my old habit of pleasure wakened, which I will keep down the more hereafter, for I thank God these pleasures are not sweet to me now in the very enjoying of them.

Samuel Pepys, diary entry, October 20, 1662

NINE

GRAVY

On Life Anew

No other word will do. For that's what it was. Gravy.
Gravy, these past ten years.
Alive, sober, working, loving and
being loved by a good woman. Eleven years
ago he was told he had six months to live
at the rate he was going. And he was going
nowhere but down. So he changed his ways
somehow....

Raymond Carver

Raymond Carver, the master American short story writer of the late twentieth century, called it his "second life"—the period between when he gave up drinking at age forty and his death ten years later from lung cancer.

Carver's wife, the poet Tess Gallagher, described it this way: "Instead of dying from alcohol, Raymond Carver chose to live," and observed that, because of his decision, he was around to see himself hailed as the literary icon he had always hoped to become.

"It took him only the wounded grace of moments-added-to-moments to inch his way free," she said. Carver considered sobriety his greatest achievement. "I'm prouder of that, that I've quit drinking, than I am of anything in my life," he told the *Paris Review*.

Just as every life is different, so every sober life is different. Perhaps, now that you've foresworn whatever substance you abused, the urge is gone, and your days are free of the addiction that once held you. It's a distant, unpleasant country you once dwelled in, didn't like, and happily left. You are never going back. The odds of you suddenly blundering there, back to the place you didn't like and don't want to return to, are nonexistent. The honest truth is you don't think about it too much. Consider yourself extraordinarily lucky.

More likely your sobriety has its ups and downs—days of joyous normalcy, busy with a dozen other things that aren't recovery; your sobriety, a pole star, the True North on your personal compass, that peak you're happily hiking toward. Other days, the work is immediate and frantic, like repairing a roof that has started to leak during a downpour: scrambling to find buckets and professional roofers. Maybe you go to meetings, regularly or now and then, to keep yourself grounded in the place you need to be, to draw energy from your fellow alcoholics. Maybe meetings are your church, your family, and you go every day.

Perhaps it's worse; perhaps the thing still howls in the cell you've put it into, some days more than others. Maybe the present seems a smoldering ruin of the past; the holidays roll around and the wine comes out and you quietly sigh and remember how nice it used to be, how diminished it is now. That's going to happen, now and then.

So you remind yourself, yet again: don't tell just pieces of the tale, but the whole story. You might yearn for the occasional return—the festive dinner, the covert hit. But it was never just one. Always remember the chain of compulsion that follows—not for everybody, but for you, and you are the only person you're in charge of. You stopped because otherwise there is no end to it. You can't drink your way to satiety. There isn't enough booze in the world. All your years of drinking didn't satisfy you. The only end is stopping and staying stopped.

You have to remind yourself to look at what you've got and not at what you haven't got. You don't dwell on other losses in your life. You don't regret giving up the violin in junior high school, or at least don't regret it much—because you aren't obsessed with the violin. You are obsessed with booze, however, or drugs, and the passing years only mute that obsession, if you're lucky. It's still there, sleeping. You have to realize that these regrets are the last after-echoes of your addiction, the Thing That Was So Important scratching at its coffin lid.

Let it scratch. Don't listen. Focus not on what you've lost but on what you've gained. The rich, full life. The pleasures of the mind—maybe even the pleasures of some of the writers you've met here. Your physical body, unscourged by addiction, able to exercise, to explore nature. The joy of simply being alive. Thousands of Americans died in drunk-driving crashes last year and tens of thousands from alcohol-related illnesses. You were not one of them. But always remember—thousands more will die driving drunk *next* year, while tens of thousands will perish from cirrhosis and strokes and other booze-borne illnesses. And the year after, and the year after that.

But your story will continue. Keep working on your life, your comedy—a "comedy," in its classical definition, being any tale that begins sadly and ends happily.

Raymond Carver ends his poem:

> ...He quit drinking! And the rest?
> After that it was *all* gravy, every minute
> of it, up to and including when he was told about,
> well, some things that were breaking down and
> building up inside his head. "Don't weep for me,"
> he said to his friends. "I'm a lucky man.
> I've had ten years longer than I or anyone
> expected. Pure gravy. And don't forget it."

The poem is inscribed on his tombstone, and recovering alcoholics and addicts often visit his grave and leave notes of thanks to Carver for his inspiration.

This is a hard road you're on. Many people, to their misfortune, couldn't do it. Many wouldn't even try. They'd rather die, and do. But you did try—at least for today, with perhaps a good feeling about tomorrow. Nothing more can be asked of life, which is so uncertain, even for those unencumbered by this most perverse of difficulties. The wisdom that helped get you here remains, always available. You have this book and whatever powerful thoughts you collect on your own. Things that are true remain true. This ordeal, so unwelcome when it occurred, might eventually become the thing of which you are most proud. To have achieved this humble rejoining of the human race, where you belong. Look at the people you know—they don't drink constantly. They don't take drugs. And now you are one of them, at least on the surface, aware of the risks and pitfalls, aware of what you must do to keep on the path.

"The world is all gates," said Ralph Waldo Emerson. "All opportunities." Take the delights and the difficulties as they come. Whether you believe each one of us is but a brief flash of light between two cold and dark eternities, or whether you believe you are climbing the stairs with Dante and Virgil toward the celestial gates of heaven, a new day awaits you.

•

what matters most is
how well you
walk through the
fire.

Charles Bukowski, "how is your heart?"

•

The deed took all my heart.
I did not think of you,
Not till the thing was done.
I put my sword away,
And then no more the cold
And perfect fury ran
Along my narrow bones,
And then no more the black
And dripping corridors
Held anywhere the shape
That I had come to slay.
Then, for the first time,
I saw in the cave's belly
The dark and clotted webs,
The green and sucking pools,
The rank and crumbling walls,
The maze of passages.

And I thought then
Of the far earth,
Of the spring sun
And the slow wind,
And a young girl.

And I looked then
At the white thread.

Hunting the minotaur
I was no common man
And had no need of love.
I trailed the shining thread
Behind me, for a vow,
And did not think of you.
It lay there, like a sign.
Coiled on the bull's great hoof
And back into the world.
Half blind with weariness
I touched the thread and wept.
O, it was frail as air.

And I turned then
With the white spool
Through the cold rocks,
Through the black rocks,
Through the long webs,
And the mist fell,

And the webs clung,
And the rocks tumbled,
and the earth shook.

And the thread held.

Mary Oliver, "The Return"

•

We know it is close
to something lofty.
Simply getting over being sick
or finding lost property
has in it the leap,
the purge, the quick humility
of witnessing a birth —
how love seeps up
and retakes the earth.
There is a dreamy
wading feeling to your walk
inside the current
of restored riches,
clocks set back,
disasters averted.

Kay Ryan, "Relief"

•

As painful as my addictions have been, they would have been even more painful had I not learned anything from them, but fortunately I have. First, you can get away with treating many things lightly in your life but your health is not one of them. As religiously as I drank and took pills, that's how religiously I gave them up. I used my addictive personality and channeled it toward diet and exercise.

Sid Caesar, *Caesar's Hours*

•

My holy of holies is the human body, health, intelligence, talent, inspiration, love, and the most absolute freedom—freedom from violence and lies, no matter what form the latter two take.

Anton Chekhov, letter to Alexis Pleshcheev, October 4, 1888

•

The life back then is gone just as surely—it's as remote to me as if it had happened to somebody I read about in a nineteenth-century novel.

Raymond Carver, interview, *Paris Review*

•

He must not doubt about it. When one doubts as to pleasure, we know what will be the conclusion. I now no more think of drinking wine than a horse does. The wine upon the table is no more for me, than for the dog that is under the table.

Samuel Johnson, quoted in *The Life of Samuel Johnson*

•

The pain was like burning or drowning, and it went on and on, unbearable. I wanted to faint, to leave my body. When you can't bear something but it goes on anyway, the person who survives isn't you anymore; you've changed and become someone else, a new person, the one who did bear it after all.

Austin Grossman, *Soon I Will Be Invincible*

9

•

I learned very early in life that the absolute worst thing
can happen to you and you will get past it and you will be
happy again.

Chuck Close, "Note to Self"

•

You have those memories but they're over. Those days are
long gone. The truth is I had great fun with drugs and alcohol for a lot of years — and then I didn't. You want to wake
up in the morning and not feel sick and wincing at what
happened the night before. Thank God, that doesn't happen anymore. Now I'm woken up by my kid's foot in my
face.

Edie Falco, interview, *The Daily Beast*

•

Listen: there's a hell
of a good universe next door; let's go.

E. E. Cummings, "pity this monster, manunkind"

•

"Carpe diem" doesn't mean seize the day — it means something gentler and more sensible. "Carpe diem" means
pluck the day. Carpe, pluck. Seize the day would be "cape
diem," if my school Latin serves. No R. Very different piece
of advice. What Horace had in mind was that you should
gently pull on the day's stem, as if it were, say, a wildflower
or an olive, holding it with all the practiced care of your

thumb and the side of your finger, which knows how to not crush easily crushed things.... Pluck the cranberry or blueberry of the day tenderly free without damaging it, is what Horace meant—pick the day, harvest the day, reap the day, mow the day, forage the day.

Nicholson Baker, *The Anthologist*

•

The key factor is the environment, whether you are talking about humans or rats. The rats that keep pressing the lever for cocaine are the ones who are stressed out because they've been raised in solitary conditions and have no other options. But when you enrich their environment, and give them access to sweets and let them play with other rats, they stop pressing the lever.

Carl Hart, Psychology Department, Columbia University

•

 The dead drug leaves a ghost behind. At certain hours it haunts the house.

Jean Cocteau, *Opium*

•

Thus, when reading in my deck-chair or when talking with others, practically any mention of any part of the world I knew instantly aroused the connotation of drinking and good fellows. Big nights and days and moments, all purple passages and freedoms, thronged my memory. "Venice" stares at me from the printed page, and I remember the café tables on the sidewalks.... And so I pondered my problem. I should not care to revisit all these fair places of the world except in the fashion I visited them before. *Glass in hand*!

Jack London, *John Barleycorn*

.

A few days later, we packed up and left. We felt good. We stopped outside Nantucket town for blueberry pancakes. This had been a farewell breakfast for us for years. The trip back to Darien was easy. I dropped the kids at the house and they helped me unload the stuff. I hugged them good-bye. Then I was off into the night. As I drove down the Hutchinson River Parkway, I had a sudden urge to turn off at the Harrison exit and drive over to the Playland amusement park, where I would buy a bottle of rum and demolish it aboard the roller coaster, screaming wildly and happily with every swoop and turn, and staying aboard until it closed down for the night. But I resisted that temptation and drove to the city. The next day, I went back to work at the advertising agency, safe and sound.

John F. Murray, "O'Phelan Drinking"

.

A man should cultivate his mind so as to have that confidence and readiness without wine, which wine gives.

Samuel Johnson, quoted in *The Life of Samuel Johnson*

•

your life is your life
don't let it be clubbed into dank
submission.
be on the watch.
there are ways out.
there is a light somewhere.
it may not be much light but
it beats the
darkness.
be on the watch.
the gods will offer you
chances.
know them, take them.
you can't beat death but
you can beat death
in life,
sometimes.
and the more often you
learn to do it,
the more light there will
be.
your life is your life.
know it while you have
it.
you are marvelous.
the gods wait to delight
in
you.

Charles Bukowski, "the laughing heart"

●

You can't really be too concerned with what people think of you. You're on your own adventure of growth and discovery. Like Charles Bukowski said, "People think I'm down on Fifth and Main at the Blarney Stone, throwing back shooters and smoking a cigar, but really I'm on the top floor of the health club with a towel in my lap, watching Johnny Carson." So it's not always good to be where people think you are, especially if you subscribe to it as well... which is easily done, because then you don't have to figure out who you are, you just ask somebody else.

Tom Waits, quoted in *Lowside of the Road*

●

Life, although it may only be an accumulation of anguish, is dear to me, and I will defend it.

Mary Shelley, *Frankenstein*

●

I don't know Who—or what—put the question, I don't know when it was put. I don't even remember answering. But at some moment I did answer *Yes* to Someone—or Something—and from that hour I was certain that existence is meaningful and that, therefore, my life, in self-surrender, had a goal.

Dag Hammarskjöld, *Markings*

•

The world is a fine place and worth the fighting for.

Ernest Hemingway, *For Whom the Bell Tolls*

•

The mind is malleable. Our life can be greatly transformed by even a minimal change in how we manage our thoughts and perceive and interpret the world. Happiness is a skill. It requires effort and time.

Matthieu Ricard, "The Happiest Man in the World?"

•

Sometimes I wish I were still out
on the back porch, drinking jet fuel
with the boys, getting louder and louder
as the empty cans drop out of our paws
like booster rockets falling back to Earth

and we soar up into the summer stars.
Summer. The big sky river rushes overhead,
bearing asteroids and mist, blind fish
and old space suits with skeletons inside.
On Earth, men celebrate their hairiness,

and it is good, a way of letting life
out of the box, uncapping the bottle
to let the effervescence gush
through the narrow, usually constricted neck.

And now the crickets plug in their appliances
in unison, and then the fireflies flash
dots and dashes in the grass, like punctuation
for the labyrinthine, untrue tales of sex
someone is telling in the dark, though

no one really hears. We gaze into the night
as if remembering the bright unbroken planet
we once came from
to which we will never
be permitted to return.
We are amazed how hurt we are.
We would give anything for what we have.

Tony Hoagland, "Jet"

·

it's good not to drink
it's good not to piss
in the sink & it's good
not to think

the clarion ring
of a glass clinking
with ice good to hear it
fade into a past
you can't sing

your dumb blues
is over. admit
it was always
borrowed. you paid
no dues you did
no time

but the time spent
sodden. what you thought
I think. your
higher power's
drunk. god's
the biggest alky
in the sky

the clouds are whiskey
sours passing by

Maureen N. McLane, "Every Day a Shiny Bright New Day"

•

I have many fond memories of the narcotics life. There's
an extreme intensity to it that, like being in combat, can't
be understood except by those who have undergone it. I
wouldn't wish addiction on anyone, but there's something
glorious about it, in a sad way.

Richard Hell, *I Dreamed I Was a Very Clean Tramp*

•

 It's better to burn out than to fade away.

Neil Young, "My My, Hey Hey (Out of the Blue)"

●

It's better to fade away like an old soldier than to burn out
... I worship the people who survive ... I'll take the living
and the healthy.

John Lennon, interview, *Playboy*

●

Through loyalty to the past, our mind refuses to realize
that tomorrow's joy is possible only if today's makes way
for it; that each wave owes the beauty of its line only to the
withdrawal of the preceding one.

André Gide, journal entry

●

Not drinking is no easy passport to happiness, no auto-
matic assurance of a good and happy and creative life.
What it *does* do is to increase the odds enormously.

Upton Sinclair, *The Cup of Fury*

●

I urge you to please notice when you are happy, and ex-
im or murmur or think at some point, "If this isn't nice,
on't know what is."

Kurt Vonnegut, *A Man without a Country*

•

won't you celebrate with me
what i have shaped into
a kind of life? i had no model.
born in babylon
both nonwhite and woman
what did i see to be except myself?
i made it up
here on this bridge between
starshine and clay,
my one hand holding tight
my other hand; come celebrate
with me that everyday
something has tried to kill me
and has failed.

Lucille Clifton, "won't you celebrate with me"

•

Looking out over the whole darn countryside, a beacon
   of satisfaction
I am. I'll not trade places with a king. Here I am then,
   continuing but ever beginning
My perennial voyage, into new memories, new hope and
   flowers
The way the coasts glide past you. I shall never forget this
   moment.

Because it consists of purest ecstasy. I am happier now
    than I ever dared believe
Anyone could be. And we finger down the dog-eared
    coasts....
It is all passing! It is past! No, I am here,
Bellow the coasts, and even the heavens roar their assent

        John Ashbery, "The Skaters"

             •

JOHNSON: No, Sir; wine gives not light, gay, ideal hilarity; but tumultuous, noisy, clamorous merriment. I have heard none of those drunken — nay drunken is a coarse word — none of those *vinous* flights.

SIR JOSHUA: Because you have sat by, quite sober, and felt an envy of the happiness of those who were drinking.

JOHNSON: Perhaps contempt.

        James Boswell, *The Life of Samuel Johnson*

             •

You think when you wake up in the mornin yesterday dont count. But yesterday is all that does count. What else is there? Your life is made out of the days it's made out of. Nothin else. You might think you could run away and change your name and I don't know what all. Start over. And then one mornin you wake up and look at the ceilin and guess who's layin there?

        Cormac McCarthy, *No Country for Old Men*

•

Imagine you wake up
with a second chance: The blue jay
hawks his pretty wares
and the oak still stands, spreading
glorious shade. If you don't look back,

the future never happens.
How good to rise in sunlight,
in the prodigal smell of biscuits—
eggs and sausage on the grill.
The whole sky is yours

to write on, blown open
to a blank page. Come on,
shake a leg! You'll never know
who's down there, frying those eggs,
if you don't get up and see.

Rita Dove, "Dawn Revisited"

•

There isn't a soul on this earth who can say for sure that
their fight with dope is over until they're dead.

Billie Holiday, *Lady Sings the Blues*

•

I caution you as I was never cautioned:

you will never let go, you will never be satiated.
You will be damaged and scarred, you will continue to hunger.

Louise Glück, "The Sensual World"

•

9

So with men's dispositions; some are pliable and easy to manage, but others have to be laboriously wrought out by hand, so to speak, and are wholly employed in the making of their own foundations. I should accordingly deem more fortunate the man who has never had any trouble with himself; but the other, I feel, has deserved better of himself, who has won a victory over the meanness of his own nature, and has not greatly led himself, but has wrestled his way, to wisdom.

Seneca, Epistle 52

•

Part of the process of recovering from my long sickness was to find delight in little things, in things unconnected with books and problems, in play, in games of tag in the swimming pool, in flying kites, in fooling with horses, in working out mechanical puzzles.

Jack London, *John Barleycorn*

•

Now there is one thing I can tell you: you will enjoy certain pleasures you would not fathom now.

Marcel Proust, letter to Georges de Lauris

•

One of the secrets of a happy life is continuous small treats.

Iris Murdoch, *The Sea, the Sea*

•

Living beings, in turning a corner, or in producing the movements required to enter the crack in a certain partially opened door, are endowed with certain properties, something which produces its own little river. These daily movements are repeated, and a certain tendency—a certain current if you will—is generated. Then this minor current, because it is a current, must at some point flow into a larger river.

Takashi Hiraide, *The Guest Cat*

•

How we spend our days is, of course, how we spend our lives. What we do with this hour, and that one, is what we are doing. A schedule defends from chaos and whim. It is a net for catching days. It is a scaffolding on which a worker can stand and labor with both hands at sections of time. A schedule is a mock-up of reason and order—willed, faked, and so brought into being; it is a peace and a haven set into the wreck of time; it is a lifeboat on which you find yourself, decades later, still living. Each day is the same, so you remember the series afterward as a blurred and powerful pattern.

Annie Dillard, *The Writing Life*

•

Sooner or later, it just becomes your life.

Bruce Springsteen, "Straight Time"

.

I'm awake; I am in the world—
I expect
no further assurance.
No protection, no promise.

Solace of the night sky,
the hardly moving
face of the clock.

I'm alone—all
my riches surround me.
I have a bed, a room.
I have a bed, a vase
of flowers beside it.
And a nightlight, a book.

I'm awake; I am safe.
The darkness like a shield, the dreams
put off, maybe
vanished forever.

And the day—
the unsatisfying morning that says
I am your future,
here is your cargo of sorrow:

Do you reject me? Do you mean
to send me away because I am not
full, in your word,
because you see
the black shape already implicit?

I will never be banished. I am the light,
your personal anguish and humiliation.
Do you dare
send me away as though
you were waiting for something better?

There is no better.
Only (for a short space)
the night sky like
a quarantine that set you
apart from your task.

Only (softly, fiercely)
the stars shining. Here,
in the room, the bedroom.
Saying *I was brave, I resisted,*
I set myself on fire.

Louise Glück, "Stars"

•

AUNT MAE: He knows a hero when he sees one.... Lord knows, kids like Henry need a hero: courageous, self-sacrificing people, setting examples for all of us. Everybody loves a hero, people line up for 'em, cheer 'em, scream their names, and years later they'll tell how they stood in the rain for hours, just to get a glimpse of the one who taught them to *hold on* a second longer. I believe there's a hero in all of us. That keeps us honest. Gives us strength. Makes us noble, and finally allows us to die with pride. Even though sometimes we have to be steady, and give up the thing we want the most.

Alvin Sargent, *Spider-Man 2*

•

Everything that happens, including humiliations, embarrassments, misfortunes, all has been given like clay, like material for one's art. One must accept it. For this reason I speak in a poem of the ancient food of heroes: humiliation, unhappiness, discord. Those things are given to us to transform, so that we may make from the miserable circumstances of our lives things that are eternal, or aspire to be so.

Jorge Luis Borges, "Blindness"

•

We experience pain and difficulty as failure instead of saying, I will pass through this, everyone I have ever admired has passed through this, music has come out of this, literature has come out of it. We should think of our humanity as a privilege.

Marilynne Robinson, *Paris Review*

•

You have been as brave as anybody I've known, and it is comforting to think about it. You probably don't think of yourself as brave because nobody who really has courage does.

Marlon Brando, letter to Tennessee Williams, May 24, 1955

•

... the Ryoan-ji rock garden in Kyoto: wherever in it a person stands, one of the fifteen rocks cannot be seen. The garden's positioned stones remind us there is always something unknowable and invisible beyond what can be perceived or comprehended, yet as real as any other rock amid the raked gravel.

Jane Hirshfield, "Thoreau's Hound: On Hiddenness"

•

You have led me from my bondage and set me free
By all those roads, by all those loving means.
That lay within your power and charity

Dante Alighieri, *Paradiso*

•

 I live soberly because I have a chance to. I drank in the past because I did not know how to do otherwise.

Vincent van Gogh, letter to his brother Theo, July 6, 1889

•

 A man goes far to find out what he is—

Theodore Roethke, "In a Dark Time"

•

As you set out for Ithaka
hope the voyage is a long one,
full of adventure, full of discovery.
Laistrygonians and Cyclops,
angry Poseidon—don't be afraid of them:
you'll never find things like that on your way
as long as you keep your thoughts raised high,
as long as a rare excitement
stirs your spirit and your body.

Laistrygonians and Cyclops,
wild Poseidon—you won't encounter them
unless you bring them along inside your soul,
unless your soul sets them up in front of you.

Hope the voyage is a long one.
May there be many a summer morning when,
with what pleasure, what joy,
you come into harbors seen for the first time;
may you stop at Phoenician trading stations
to buy fine things,
mother of pearl and coral, amber and ebony,
sensual perfume of every kind—
as many sensual perfumes as you can;
and may you visit many Egyptian cities
to gather stores of knowledge from their scholars.

Keep Ithaka always in your mind.
Arriving there is what you are destined for.
But do not hurry the journey at all.
Better if it lasts for years,
so you are old by the time you reach the island,
wealthy with all you have gained on the way,
not expecting Ithaka to make you rich.

Ithaka gave you the marvelous journey.
Without her you would not have set out.
She has nothing left to give you now.

And if you find her poor, Ithaka won't have fooled you.
Wise as you will have become, so full of experience,
you will have understood by then what these Ithakas mean.

Constantine P. Cavafy, "Ithaka"

•

"Kindness" covers all of my political beliefs. No need to spell them out. I believe that if, at the end, according to our abilities, we have done something to make others a little happier, and something to make ourselves a little happier, that is about the best we can do. To make others less happy is a crime. To make ourselves unhappy is where all crime starts. We must try to contribute joy to the world. That is true no matter what our problems, our health, our circumstances. We must try. I didn't always know this and am happy I lived long enough to find it out.

Roger Ebert, *Life Itself*

•

For us, there is only the trying. The rest is not our business.

T. S. Eliot, "East Coker"

•

Another opportunity was given you — as a favor and as a burden. The question is not: why did it happen this way, or where is it going to lead you, or what is the price you will have to pay. It is simply: *how* are you making use of it.

Dag Hammarskjöld, *Markings*

•

But what could you do? Only keep going. People kept going; they had been doing it for thousands of years. You took the kindness offered, letting it seep as far in as it could go, and the remaining dark crevices you carried around

with you, knowing that over time they might change into
something almost bearable.

Elizabeth Strout, *Amy and Isabelle*

9

•

... I believe in intention and I believe in work. I believe in
waking up in the middle of the night and packing our bags
and leaving our worst selves for our better ones.

Leslie Jamison, "The Empathy Exams"

•

The world breaks everyone and afterward many are strong
at the broken places.

Ernest Hemingway, *A Farewell to Arms*

•

And once the storm is over you won't remember how you
made it through, how you managed to survive. You won't
even be sure, in fact, whether the storm is really over. But
one thing is certain. When you come out of the storm you
won't be the same person who walked in. That's what this
storm's all about.

Haruki Murakami, *Kafka on the Shore*

There's still time to change things.

Siri Hustvedt, *The Blazing World*

ACKNOWLEDGMENTS

We would like to thank John Tryneski, executive editor of the University of Chicago Press, for taking a chance with an unconventional book, then seeing it through to completion. Thanks to everyone at the press who labored to bring it into being, but particularly Rodney Powell, who cheerfully took on the difficult, complicated, and seemingly endless task of handling the extensive legal permissions required. This book would not exist in its present form without his tireless, skillful, and diligent efforts. Thanks as well to publicity director Ellen Gibson, who first brought the book to the press's attention, Yvonne Zipter, for her thorough and meticulous reading of the text, and June Sawyers for the index.

This book would not have been possible without the financial support of generous individuals whose donations have helped to cover the substantial fees required to reprint many of the poems, song lyrics, and other copyrighted material used in the text. Our profound gratitude to Beverly and Lawrence Bader, Claudine Bing, Sue Erikson Bloland, Rosemary Booth and Gerald O'Leary, Eleni and Jimmy Bousis, Grant DePorter, Harve A. Ferrill, Michael Ferro, Lee Flaherty, Laura and Martin Gardner, Sylvia and David Hammerman, Leslie Hindman, Sidney and Shirley Horowitz, Blair Hull, Sheila and Hy Kempler,

Maria LoBalbo, Tassos Loumis, Rich Melman, Lita Moses and Bruce Bernstein, Harriet and Howard Pollock, Richard S. Price, Bruce Sagan, Carol and Theodore Steinman, and those who wish to remain anonymous.

Annasophia Loumis, Ron Magers, and Hedy Ratner also provided valuable guidance for this process.

Much of the permission seeking was done online, but at times we communicated with the artists or their estates directly and some rights' holders responded with unusual kindness. Thanks to the generosity of Jane Hirshfield, Clancy Martin, Maureen N. McLane, Frank Orrall, Robert Pinsky, Kay Ryan, Rosemary Thurber, and Michael Timmins. Savannah Lake at the Wylie Agency went beyond the call of duty to help us, as did Ron Hussey at Houghton Mifflin.

Judy Collins, Molly Keelan, Dr. Walter Ling, Edie Steinberg, Alexandra Styron, and Joe W. offered valuable feedback during the writing process.

Our stellar agent, Susan Raihofer, of the David Black Literary Agency, provided much appreciated enthusiasm and encouragement throughout.

Thank you.

SOURCE NOTES

INTRODUCTION

x   **"If you had a sty"** Horace, *The Epistles of Horace*, trans. David Ferry (New York: Farrar, Straus and Giroux, 2002), 15.

xi   **"Let us posit as a given"** Dante Alighieri, *Purgatorio*, trans. Jean Hollander and Robert Hollander (New York: Doubleday, 2003), canto 18, line 70, 367.

xi   **"Other people's words"** Zadie Smith, *Changing My Mind: Occasional Essays* (New York: Penguin, 2009), 102.

xii   **"Are the dangling threads"** Geoffrey O'Brien, "We Are What We Quote," *New York Times*, March 3, 2013, 9.

xii   **"Better I should know"** Sarah McLachlan, "Fallen," on *Afterglow* (Sony/ATV Songs LLC/Tyde Music, USA, 2003).

xii   **"Yield not to evils"** Virgil, *The Aeneid*, trans. E. Fairfax Taylor (London: J. M. Dent, 1903), 139. **"But go forth all the bolder to face them"** Virgil, *The Aeneid*, trans. H. R. Fairclough (Cambridge, MA: Loeb Classical Library, Harvard University Press, 1916), 539.

xii   **"For the past was dream"** Robert Browning, "Ixion," *The Complete Works of Robert Browning* (Boston: Houghton, Mifflin, 1899), 208.

xiii   **"Generally behaved myself"** Edith Wharton, letter, in *My Dear Governess: The Letters of Edith Wharton to Anna Bahlmann*, ed. Irene Goldman-Price (New Haven, CT: Yale University Press, 2012), 37.

xiii   **"Recovery is possible"** Saul Bellow, *Seize the Day* (New York: Penguin, 2001), 78.

CHAPTER ONE

2   **"Man, being reasonable"** Lord George Gordon Byron, *Don Juan*, in *The Works of Lord Byron: Including the Suppressed Poems* (Philadelphia: Lippincott, 1856), 589, verse 179.

3 **"Mistake their private ail"** Henry Thoreau, *The Correspondence of Henry D. Thoreau, 1834–48*: 1. (Princeton, NJ: Princeton University Press, 2013), 250.

4 **"But to return"** Byron, *Don Juan*, verses 179–80.

4 **"You don't decide"** William S. Burroughs, *Junky* (New York: Grove Press, 2003), 5.

4 **"It was not always"** Rainer Maria Rilke, *A Year with Rilke*, trans. Joanna Macy and Anita Barrows (New York: HarperOne, 2009), 318.

6 **"All ways led"** Jack London, *John Barleycorn* (London: Mills & Boon, 1914), 5.

6 **"At a tavern"** Samuel Johnson, in James Boswell, *The Life of Samuel Johnson, LL.D.* (New York: Heritage Press, 1963), 2:240.

6 **"Bring in the bottled lightning"** Charles Dickens, *The Life and Adventures of Nicholas Nickleby* (London: Chapman and Hall, 1839), 489.

6 **"A martini makes"** Anaïs Nin, diary entry, in *The Diary of Anaïs Nin: 1947–1955* (New York: Harcourt Brace Jovanovich, 1975), 118.

7 **"What beauty can compare"** Malcolm Lowry, *Under the Volcano* (New York: HarperPerennial, 2007), 52.

7 **"all the best of life"** Robert Lowell, "For John Berryman," in *Collected Poems*, ed. Frank Bidart and David Gewanter (New York: Farrar, Straus and Giroux, 2003), 737.

7 **"On a busy night"** Mark Stevens and Annalyn Swan, *de Kooning: An American Master* (New York: Knopf, 2004), 361.

7 **"In places where drinks"** Simone de Beauvoir, *America Day by Day*, trans. Carol Cosman (Berkeley: University of California Press, 1999), 16.

8 **"Most of those at the Algonquin"** Anne Roiphe, *Art and Madness: A Memoir of Lust without Reason* (New York: Doubleday, 2011), 116–17.

8 **"Give me a bowl of wine"** William Shakespeare, "The Tragedy of Richard the Third," in *The Riverside Shakespeare*, 2nd ed. (Boston: Houghton Mifflin, 1997), 1:790.

8 **"if the storm within"** Vincent van Gogh, letter to his brother Theo, in *The Complete Letters of Vincent van Gogh: With Reproductions of All the Drawings in the Correspondence* (New York: New York Graphic Society, 1958), 2:619.

9 **"Only a drink"** Eugene O'Neill, letter to his wife, in *Selected Letters of Eugene O'Neill*, ed. Travis Bogard and Jackson R. Bryer (New York: Proscenium, 1994), 114.

9 **"I can't seem to get used to myself"** Eugene Ionesco, *Rhinoceros and Other Plays* (New York: Grove Press, 1960), 18.

9 **"Now he was feeling just swell"** Charles Jackson, *The Lost Weekend* (New York: Random House, 2013), 74.

9–10 **"You can show me no man"** Seneca, Epistle 37, in *Epistles: 1–65*, trans. Richard M. Gummere (Boston: Harvard University Press, 1917), 257.

10   **"Voluntarily or involuntarily"** Bertrand Russell, *The Conquest of Happiness* (Oxon: Routledge, 1993), 46.

10   **"Well, my self-consciousness"** Bill Wilson, quoted in *Bill W. and Mr. Wilson: The Legend and Life of A.A.'s Cofounder,* by Matthew J. Raphael (Amherst: University of Massachusetts Press, 2000), 41.

10–11 **"Shooting was thrilling"** Etta James and David Ritz, *Rage to Survive: The Etta James Story* (New York: Da Capo Press, 2003), 108.

11   **"We have faith"** Arthur Rimbaud, "Drunken Morning," in *Arthur Rimbaud: Complete Works,* trans. Paul Schmidt (New York: Harper Perennial Modern Classics, 2008), 255–56.

11   **"So I go and get another beer"** Thomas Merton, *Learning to Love: Exploring Solitude and Freedom,* vol. 6 of *Journals of Thomas Merton* (San Francisco: HarperSanFrancisco, 1997), 340.

11   **"Though I never took a drink"** Sid Caesar, *Caesar's Hours: My Life in Comedy, with Love and Laughter* (New York: PublicAffairs, 2003), 263.

12   **"I found the tide of wine"** Washington Irving, *The Keeping of Christmas at Bracebridge Hall* (New York: Dutton, 1906), 61.

12   **"I leave my typewriter"** John Cheever, letter to Josephine Herbst, in *The Letters of John Cheever,* ed. Benjamin Cheever (New York: Simon and Schuster, 1988), 262–63.

12–13 **"When I got back to Los Angeles"** Charles Bukowski, *Factotum* (Santa Rosa, CA: Black Sparrow Press, 1975), 66–67.

13   **"Lately I've been"** Philip Levine, "Words," in *New Selected Poems* (New York: Knopf, 1991), 193–94.

14   **"How on earth do I know"** Tennessee Williams, *Notebooks* (New Haven, CT: Yale University Press, 2006), 703.

14   **"It's not the folly of foolishness"** Horace, *Epistles of Horace,* trans. David Ferry (New York: Farrar, Straus and Giroux, 2002), 65.

CHAPTER TWO

16   **"I'll just stop in"** James Thurber, "One Is a Wanderer," in *The Thurber Carnival* (New York: Harper & Bros., 1945), 164.

17   **"I think maybe"** Ibid., 167.

17   **"That's the way alcoholism works"** Caroline Knapp, *Drinking: A Love Story* (New York: Dial Press, 1997), 108.

18   **"I achieved a condition"** Jack London, *John Barleycorn* (London: Mills & Boon, 1914), 267.

18   **"This I take"** Ibid., 254.

18   **"I decided; I shall take"** Ibid., 305.

20   **"Drugs are a carnival"** Edith Piaf, quoted in Simone Berteaut *Piaf: A Biography* (New York: Harper & Row, 1972), 391.

20 **"There was nothing to do"** Ernest Hemingway, discarded first chapters of *The Sun Also Rises* (New York: Simon and Schuster, 2014), app. 3, 275. Item 202 of the Ernest Hemingway Collection, John F. Kennedy Library, Boston.

20 **"God, how pointless"** Malcolm Lowry, *Under the Volcano* (New York: Harper Perennial Modern Classics, 2007), 360.

20–21 **"I had a straight shot"** Raymond Carver, "Luck," in *All of Us: The Collected Poems* (New York: Alfred A. Knopf, 1998), 3–5.

21 **"More, more, I think"** M. F. K. Fisher, "G Is for Gluttony," in *An Alphabet for Gourmets* (New York: Macmillan, 1989), 50.

21 **"But the same stimulus"** London, *John Barleycorn*, 244.

21–22 **"As for quenching"** Charles Jackson, *The Lost Weekend* (New York: Random House, 2013), 41.

22 **"Vices are never genuinely tamed"** Seneca, Epistle 85, in *Epistles: 66–92*, trans. Richard M. Gummere (Boston: Harvard University Press, 1920), 291.

22 **"After two drinks"** Mark Stevens and Annalyn Swan, *de Kooning: An American Master* (New York: Knopf, 2004), 365.

22–23 **"He and Al Shockley"** Stephen King, *The Shining* (New York: Anchor, 2012), 155–56.

23 **"He began to grow disgusted"** David Foster Wallace, *Infinite Jest* (New York: Back Bay Books, 2006), 21–22.

23 **"What time is it?"** Seth Mnookin, "Harvard and Heroin," *Salon*, August 27, 1999. http://www.salon.com/1999/08/27/heroinson/.

24 **"I don't want you to think"** Billy Wilder and I. A. L. Diamond (screenplay); Billy Wilder (director), *Some Like It Hot*, distributed by United Artists, 1959.

24 **"Booze will send me"** Geoffrey Wolff, *A Day at the Beach: Recollections* (New York: Alfred A. Knopf, 1992), 100.

24 **"You cannot selectively numb"** Brené Brown, "The Power of Vulnerability," TED talk, June, 2010 Houston, Texas. https://www.youtube.com/watch?v=iCvmsMzlF70.

24–25 **"Life, friends, is boring"** John Berryman, "Life, Friends," in *The Dream Songs* (New York: Farrar, Straus and Giroux, 2007), 16.

25 **"I positively dread retirement"** Philip Larkin, letter to Judy Egerton, in *Selected Letters of Philip Larkin 1940–1985*, ed. Anthony Thwaite (New York: Farrar, Straus and Giroux, 1993), 696.

25 **"Francis felt healthy"** William Kennedy, *Ironweed* (New York: Penguin, 1984), 8.

25 **"It was at this time"** London, *John Barleycorn*, 234.

26 **"In church, on my knees"** John Cheever, *The Journals of John Cheever* (New York: Knopf, 2011), 188.

26 **"My Uncle Wight, Mr. Talbott, and others"** Samuel Pepys, diary entry, in *The Diary of Samuel Pepys*, vol. 2: *1661*, ed. Robert Latham and William Matthews (Berkeley: University of California Press, 1971), 99.

26   **"And the commencement of atonement"** Lord Byron, "Manfred," in *The Works of the Right Honourable Lord Byron* (London: John Murray, 1818), 142.

26–27 **"I realized that"** Lillian Roth, *I'll Cry Tomorrow* (New York: Frederick Fell, 1954), 132.

27   **"…it is difficult"** Dr. Vincent Felitti, "The Origins of Addiction: Evidence from the Adverse Childhood Experiences Study," 2003, http://www.nijc.org /pdfs/Subject%20Matter%20Articles/Drugs%20and%20Alc/ACE%20 Study%20-%20OriginsofAddiction.pdf.

27   **"Men sink themselves"** Seneca, Epistle 39, in *Epistles: 1–65*, 257.

28   **"For in so far as drinking"** G. K. Chesterton, *All Things Considered* (New York: John Lane, 1909), 235.

28   **"I see the better way"** Ovid, *Metamorphoses*, trans. Eugene Ehrlich, in *Amo, Amas, Amat and More*, by Eugene Ehrlich (New York: Harper & Row, 1985), 294.

28   **"I await with patience"** Albert Camus, *Notebooks, 1951–1959* (Chicago: Ivan R. Dee, 2008), 20.

28   **"How did you go bankrupt?"** Ernest Hemingway, *The Sun Also Rises* (New York: Simon and Schuster, 2002), 141.

28   **"Drinking heavily"** Jack Kerouac, *Some of the Dharma* (New York: Viking Penguin, 1999), 112.

29   **"Addiction is lonely"** Richard Hell, *I Dreamed I Was a Very Clean Tramp: An Autobiography* (New York: HarperCollins, 2013), 251–52.

29   **"I shot into the back of my hands"** John Phillips with Jim Jerome, *Papa John* (Garden City, NY: Doubleday, 1986), 318.

29   **"I wish you knew me"** Gil Scott-Heron, quoted in Alec Wilkinson, "New York Is Killing Me," *New Yorker*, August 9, 2010, 26–32.

30   **"After three quick double whiskies"** Kingsley Amis, *The Green Man* (1969; repr., New York: New York Review Books Classics, 2013), 45.

30   **"It is often tragic"** C. G. Jung, *Collected Works of C. G. Jung*, vol. 9, pt. 2: *Aion: Researches into the Phenomenology of the Self* (Princeton, NJ: Princeton University Press, 2014), 10.

30   **"At the end of my drinking"** Mary Karr, *Lit* (New York: HarperCollins, 2009), 7.

31   **"Desperation is the raw material"** William S. Burroughs, *The Western Lands* (New York: Penguin Books, 1988), 116.

31   **"I wonder if I am becoming"** Larkin, in *Selected Letters*, 722.

31   **"It was one of those midsummer"** John Cheever, "The Swimmer," in *The Stories of John Cheever* (New York: Knopf, 1978), 603.

31   **"A small note"** Sylvia Plath, journal entry, in *The Unabridged Journals of Sylvia Plath*, ed. Karen V. Kukil (New York: Knopf, 2007), 210.

32   **"Snuggling luxuriously"** Emily Hahn, "The Big Smoke," *New Yorker*, February 15, 1969, 39.

32 **"What had happened?"** Stephen King, *The Shining* (New York: Anchor Books, 2012), 75.

32 **"One day, gorgeous as usual"** Domenica Ruta, *With or Without You* (New York: Random House, 2013), 168.

33 **"The eyes that fix you"** T. S. Eliot, "The Love Song of J. Alfred Prufrock," in *Collected Poems, 1909–1962* (New York: Harcourt Brace, 1991), 5.

33 **"The delusion under which"** Rick Moody, interview by David Ryan, "The Art of Fiction No. 166," *Paris Review*, no. 158 (Spring–Summer 2001), http://www.theparisreview.org/interviews/509/the-art-of-fiction-no-166-rick-moody.

33 **"Thinking again, in the dentist's chair"** Cheever, *The Journals of John Cheever*, 5.

34 **"That night"** Sid Caesar, *Caesar's Hours: My Life in Comedy, with Love and Laughter* (New York: PublicAffairs, 2003), 261.

34 **"I have a theory"** Jeanette Winterson, *Oranges Are Not the Only Fruit* (New York: Grove Press, 1997), 169.

34 **"That Which I Should Have Done"** Ivan Albright, painting titled: *That Which I Should Have Done I Did Not Do (The Door)*, 1931–41, the Art Institute of Chicago.

34–35 **"His gaze"** Rainer Maria Rilke, "The Panther," in *A Year with Rilke*, trans. Joanna Macy and Anita Barrows (New York: HarperOne, 2009), 12.

35 **"The crack is moving"** Weldon Kees, "Five Villanelles," in *The Collected Poems of Weldon Kees*, ed. Donald Justice (Lincoln: University of Nebraska Press, 1962), 65.

35 **"Houses crack"** Seneca, Epistle 103, in *Epistles: 93–124*, trans. Richard M. Gummere (Boston: Harvard University Press, 1925), 187.

36 **"Because we lived"** Mary Oliver, "The House," in *New and Selected Poems* (1992; repr., Boston: Beacon Press, 2004), 1:244.

36–37 **"When he was in his last clinic"** Simon Gray, *The Smoking Diaries* (New York: Caroll & Graf, 2005), 1:134.

37 **"Footfalls echo"** T. S. Eliot, "Burnt Norton," in *Collected Poems, 1909–1962* (New York: Harcourt Brace, 1991), 175.

37 **"Disaster can be"** David Esterly, in *The Lost Carving: A Journey to the Heart of Making* (New York: Penguin Books, 2013), 67.

37–38 **"When the beginnings of self-destruction"** Cheever, *The Journals of John Cheever*, 23.

38 **"It is the speck"** Emily Dickinson, letter to Louise and Frances Norcross, in *The Letters of Emily Dickinson*, ed. Thomas H. Johnson (Cambridge, MA: Belknap Press of Harvard University Press, 1958), 2:490.

38 **"One doesn't discover"** André Gide, *The Counterfeiters* (New York: Knopf Doubleday, 2012), 353.

38   **"You may do this"** Jane Hirshfield, "Da Capo," in *The Lives of the Heart* (New York: HarperPerennial, 1997), 19.

CHAPTER THREE

40   **"When you are completely off balance"** Roger Rosenblatt, *Kayak Morning: Reflections on Love, Grief, and Small Boats* (New York: HarperCollins, 2012), 9.

41   **"No matter where you go . . . there you are"** Earl Mac Rauch, *The Adventures of Buckaroo Banzai across the Eighth Dimension*, directed by W. D. Richter (1984; issued on DVD, Los Angeles: Sherwood Productions, MGM, 2002).

42   **"How beautiful is candor!"** Walt Whitman, *Leaves of Grass: 150th Anniversary Edition* (New York: Oxford University Press, 2005), xi.

44   **"Rowing with just one oar"** Ko Un, in *Flowers of a Moment*, trans. Brother Anthony, Young-moo Kim, and Gary Gach (Rochester, NY: BOA Editions, 2006), 19.

44   **"Ripeness is all"** William Shakespeare, "King Lear," in *The Riverside Shakespeare*, 2nd ed. (Boston: Houghton Mifflin, 1997), 2:1339.

44   **"Sorrow is an angel"** Frank Orrall, "Complicated," recorded by Poi Dog Pondering on *Pomegranate* (Bar/None Records, 1995).

44   **"I have newly taken"** Samuel Pepys, in *The Diary of Samuel Pepys*, vol. 2: *1661*, ed. Robert Latham and William Matthews (Berkeley: University of California Press, 1971), 242.

45   **"These passions, which are heavy"** Seneca, Epistle 37, in *Epistles: 1–65*, trans. Richard M. Gummere (Boston: Harvard University Press, 1917), 255.

45   **"It's never the changes we want"** Junot Díaz, *The Brief Wondrous Life of Oscar Wao* (London: Faber and Faber, 2009), 51.

45   **"This storm irresistibly propels"** Walter Benjamin, *Illuminations*, trans. Harry Zohn (New York: Houghton Mifflin Harcourt, 1968), 258.

45   **"Well, I'm gone to Detox Mansion"** Warren Zevon and Jorge Calderón, "Detox Mansion," recorded by Warren Zevon on *Sentimental Hygiene* (Virgin Records, 1987).

46   **"Awake ye drunkards"** Quoted in *The English Bible*, vol. 4: *Isaiah to Malachi* (London: David Nutt, 1903), 302.

46   **"Wine I never thought"** Ernest Hemingway, *Selected Letters, 1917–1961*, ed. Carlos Baker (New York: Scribner, 1981), 877.

46   **"My eyes are wide open"** John Lennon, "Cold Turkey" (Apple Records, 1969).

47   **"Why, this is hell"** Christopher Marlowe, "Tragical History of Doctor Faustus," in *Old English Drama: Select Plays*, ed. Adolphus William Ward (Oxford: Clarendon Press, 1892), 10.

47   **"Will power is nothing"** John Berryman, *Recovery* (New York: Farrar, Straus and Giroux, 1973), 50.

47   **"Comforter, where, where is your comforting?"** Gerard Manley Hopkins, "No worst, there is none," in *Selected Poems of Gerard Manley Hopkins* (Mineola, NY: Dover, 2011), 54.

47–48 **"O despairer"** Whitman, *Leaves of Grass*, 54.

48   **"The gates of hell are open"** Virgil, *The Aeneid*, trans. John Dryden (Cambridge: Cambridge University Press, 1911), 66; **"But to retrace your steps"** Virgil, *The Aeneid*, trans. Robert Fagles (New York: Penguin, 2006), 186.

48   **"Any fool can get into an ocean"** Jack Spicer, *My Vocabulary Did This to Me: The Collected Poetry of Jack Spicer* (Middleton, CT: Wesleyan University Press, 2008), 23.

48–49 **"No one's a hero"** Keith Richards, *Life* (New York: Little, Brown and Company, 2010), 408.

49   **"What was it like"** Louise Glück, "Tango," in *Poems 1962–2012* (New York: Farrar, Straus and Giroux, 2012), 118.

49   **"I had not thought of myself"** Claire Messud, *The Last Life: A Novel* (New York: Harcourt, 1999), 308.

49–50 **"So this purports to be a disease"** David Foster Wallace, *Infinite Jest* (New York: Back Bay Books, 2006), 180.

50   **"To give a brief definition"** Seneca, Epistle 75, in *Epistles: 66–92*, trans. Richard M. Gummere (Boston: Harvard University Press, 1920), 143.

50   **"Healing . . . is not a science"** W. H. Auden, "The Art of Healing," in *Collected Poems*, ed. Edward Mendelson (New York: Random House, 2007), 836.

50   **"Do you not see how necessary"** John Keats, letter to George and Georgiana Keats, in *The Letters of John Keats*, ed. H. Buxton Forman (London: Reeves & Turner, 1895), 327.

50   **"Why are you so unwilling"** Steven Frisch, conversation.

51   **"These are the days"** Walt Whitman, "Song of the Open Road," in *The Portable Walt Whitman* (New York: Penguin, 2003), 146.

51   **"There is a point"** Dag Hammarskjöld, *Markings*, trans. Leif Sjöberg and W. H. Auden (New York: Knopf, 1964), 66.

51   **"What was lost was lost"** Haruki Murakami, *Hard-Boiled Wonderland and the End of the World*, trans. Alfred Birnbaum (New York: Random House, 1993), 164.

51   **"He sank so low"** Dante Alighieri, *Purgatorio*, trans. Jean Hollander and Robert Hollander (New York: Doubleday, 2003), 627.

52   **"There were about thirty guys"** Larry Hagman with Todd Gold, *Hello Darlin'* (New York: Simon and Schuster, 2001), 243.

52   **"All's misalliance"** Robert Lowell, "Epilogue," in *Robert Lowell: Selected Poems* (New York: Farrar, Straus and Giroux, 2006), 338.

53 **"I have been confined"** John Cheever, letter to Arthur Spear, in *The Letters of John Cheever*, ed. Benjamin Cheever (New York: Simon and Schuster, 1988), 312–13.

53 **"I cannot help thinking"** E. M. Forster, *A Room with a View* (Norfolk, CT: Knopf, 1922), 60.

54 **"Just this, just this"** W. S. Merwin, in *The Buddha: The Story of Siddhartha*, documentary directed by David Grubin (PBS, 2010).

54 **"It is now high time"** Marcus Aurelius, *Marcus Aurelius* (London: Arthur Humphreys, 1902), 22.

54 **"Thirty years ago my older brother"** Anne Lamott, *Bird by Bird* (New York: Anchor, 1995), 18–19.

55 **"Between where you are now"** David Bohm, quoted by F. David Peat, interviewed in "Look for Truth—No Matter Where It Takes You," http://www.fdavidpeat.com/interviews/wie.htm.

55 **"Regret is vain"** Edgar Bowers, "Amor Vincit Omnia," in *Collected Poems* (New York: Knopf, 1999), 150.

55 **"I began to be sensible of strange feelings"** Herman Melville, *Moby-Dick; or, The Whale* (New York: Harper & Bros., 1851), 56.

56 **"Your heart's in retrograde"** Kate Light, "There Comes the Strangest Moment," in *Open Slowly* (Lincoln, NE: Zoo Press, 2003), 65.

56 **"Hard is trying to rebuild yourself"** Nick Hornby, *A Long Way Down* (New York: Penguin, 2005), 322.

56 **"It's very hard to stop"** Tom Waits, quoted in Barney Hoskyns, *Lowside of the Road: A Life of Tom Waits* (London: Faber and Faber, 2009), 276.

56 **"But then one regrets the loss"** Oscar Wilde, *The Picture of Dorian Gray* (Leipzig: Bernhard Tauchnitz, 1908), 272.

57 **"At night I supped with him"** James Boswell, *The Life of Samuel Johnson LL.D.* (New York: Heritage Press, 1963), 1:360.

57–58 **"Let me begin again"** Philip Levine, "Let Me Begin Again," in *Selected Poems* (New York: Atheneum, 1984), 191.

58 **"Wave of sorrow"** Langston Hughes, "Island [1]," in *The Collected Poems of Langston Hughes* (New York: Random House, 1994), 376.

CHAPTER FOUR

60 **"Staring moodily"** John Berryman, *Recovery* (New York: Farrar, Straus and Giroux, 1973), 11.

61 **"There is no such thing"** Lord Byron, letter to Mr. Moore, in *The Life, Letters, and Journals of Lord Byron*, Thomas Moore (London: John Murray, 1866), 515.

62 **"un-numbing now"** John Berryman, "Compline," in *John Berryman Collected Poems: 1937–1971*, ed. Charles Thornbury (New York: Macmillan, 1989), 234.

64 **"When the morning's freshness"** Dag Hammarskjöld, *Markings*, trans. Leif Sjöberg and W. H. Auden (New York: Alfred A. Knopf, 1964), 124.

64 **"I feel that perhaps"** John Cheever, *The Journals of John Cheever* (New York: Knopf, 2011), 365.

64 **"I wish one could be sure"** Emily Dickinson, letter to Louise Norcross, in *The Letters of Emily Dickinson* (Boston: Harvard University Press, 1986), 407.

64 **"The wise men teach us"** Michel de Montaigne, trans. M. A. Screech, "On Solitude," in *The Essays: A Selection* (New York: Penguin, 1993), 105.

65 **"Wanting to stop"** Paul Molloy, *Where Did Everybody Go?* (Garden City, NY: Doubleday, 1981), 45.

65 **"... a cure imposed"** Keith Richards, *Life* (New York: Little, Brown and Company, 2010), 395.

65 **"Men's courses will foreshadow"** Charles Dickens, *A Christmas Carol* (London: Bradbury & Evans, 1858), 90.

65 **"At moments of departure"** Leo Tolstoy, *War and Peace*, trans. Richard Pevear and Larissa Volokhonsky (New York: Vintage Classics, 2008), 105.

65–66 **"He believed that he must"** Saul Bellow, *Seize the Day* (New York: Penguin, 2001), 78.

66 **"It may be unfair"** Khaled Hosseini, *The Kite Runner* (New York: Riverhead, 2003), 142.

66 **"People don't like it"** Ricky Gervais, Twitter, October 11, 2013.

66 **"The reawakening"** Jean Cocteau, *Opium: The Diary of a Cure*, trans. Margaret Crosland and Sinclair Road (New York: Grove Press, 1958), 25–26.

67 **"It having been"** Samuel Pepys, diary entry, in *The Diary of Samuel Pepys*, vol. 3: *1662*, ed. Robert Latham and William Matthews (Berkeley: University of California Press, 1971), 18.

67 **"Do what you can"** Hammarskjöld, *Markings*, 124.

67 **"I ... generally behaved myself"** Edith Wharton, letter, in *My Dear Governess: The Letters of Edith Wharton to Anna Bahlmann*, ed. Irene Goldman-Price (New Haven, CT: Yale University Press, 2012), 37.

67 **"Not drinking is beginning"** Robert Lowell, letter to Elizabeth Bishop, in *Words in Air: The Complete Correspondence between Elizabeth Bishop and Robert Lowell*, ed. Thomas Travisano with Saskia Hamilton (New York: Macmillan, 2010), 375.

68 **"... I'm no longer crouched"** Anne Lamott, *Grace (Eventually): Thoughts on Faith* (New York: Riverhead, 2007), 116.

68 **"BOSWELL: The great difficulty"** James Boswell, *The Life of Samuel Johnson, LL.D.* (New York: Heritage Press, 1963), 3:33–34.

69 **"For how does any man"** Nelson Algren, *The Man with the Golden Arm: 50th Anniversary Critical Edition* (New York: Seven Stories Press, 1999), 142.

69 **"O! I have suffered"** William Shakespeare, *The Tempest*, in *The Riverside Shakespeare*, 2nd ed. (Boston: Houghton Mifflin, 1997), 2:1662.

69 **"I'd like to begin again"** Deborah Garrison, "On New Terms," in *The Second Child* (New York: Random House, 2008), 3.

70 **"That Christmas he and Lee"** Deborah Solomon, *Jackson Pollock: A Biography* (New York: Cooper Square Press, 2001), 189.

70 **"You know, you never really saw"** Raymond Chandler, letter to Jessica Tyndale, in *The Raymond Chandler Papers: Selected Letters and Nonfiction, 1909–1959* (New York: Grove Press, 2002), 214.

70 **"Up the river to Yaddo"** John Cheever, *The Journals of John Cheever* (New York: Knopf, 2011), 311.

71 **"Besides, it is a certain fact"** Vincent van Gogh, letter to Mr. and Mrs. Ginoux, 1890, in *The Complete Letters of Vincent van Gogh* (Greenwich, CT: New York Graphic Society, 1958), 281.

71 **"Bird himself was wary"** Kenzaburō Ōe, *A Personal Matter*, trans. John Nathan (New York: Grove Press, 1969), 6.

71 **"How far back"** Philip Roth, "Epstein," in *The Paris Review Book for Planes, Trains, Elevators, and Waiting Rooms* (New York: Picador, 2004), 121.

71 **"There are very few"** Anaïs Nin, diary entry, in *The Diary of Anaïs Nin*, vol. 3: *1939–1944*, ed. Gunther Stuhlmann (New York: Harcourt Brace Jovanovich, 1969), 294.

72 **"You were sick"** Kurt Vonnegut, *Timequake* (New York: Berkley Books, 1998), 193.

72 **"Habit is habit"** Mark Twain, "Pudd'nhead Wilson's Calendar," in *Pudd'nhead Wilson* (Hartford, CT: American Publishing, 1897), 77.

72 **"A month now"** Lowell, *Words in Air*, 475.

72 **"To possess your soul"** Charles Edward Montague, *Disenchantment* (New York: Brentano's, 1922), 254.

73 **"You are never stronger"** Zadie Smith, *White Teeth* (New York: Vintage, 2001), 97.

73 **"I am withdrawing"** Patrick Lane, *What the Stones Remember: A Life Rediscovered* (Boston: Trumpeter Books, 2005), 4.

73 **"Listen, Truman"** John Cheever, quoted in Gerald Clarke, *Capote: A Biography* (New York: Carroll & Graf, 2001), 504.

73–74 **"My identity shifted"** Eric Clapton, interviewed by Cal Fussman, "What I've Learned: Eric Clapton," *Esquire*, January 2008.

74 **"In a time of drastic change"** Thomas Merton, *Conjectures of a Guilty Bystander* (New York: Doubleday Religion, 2009), 206.

74 **"...happiness is not something"** Mihaly Csikszentmihalyi, *Flow: The Psychology of Optimal Experience* (New York: Harper Perennial, 2008), 2.

75 **"I no longer plumb the depths"** Etty Hillesum, diary entry, in *Etty: The Letters and Diaries of Etty Hillesum, 1941–1943*, ed. Klaas A. D. Smelik, trans. Arnold J. Pomerans (Grand Rapids, MI: Wm. B. Eerdmans, 2002), 225–26.

CHAPTER FIVE

78 **"Wait, for now"** Galway Kinnell, "Wait," in *Selected Poems* (New York: Houghton Mifflin, 1982), 127.

79 **"Today we were unlucky"** from IRA statement quoted in "International News," Maureen Johnson, Associated Press, October 12, 1984.

82 **"Time off the drug"** Walter Ling, quoted in David Sheff, *Beautiful Boy: A Father's Journey through His Son's Addiction* (New York: Houghton Mifflin, 2008), 140.

84 **"Life is very long"** T. S. Eliot, "The Hollow Men," in *Selected Poems* (New York: Harcourt Brace, 1964), 80.

84 **"Barflies mortgage years"** Michael Miner, "Home Fires," *Chicago Reader*, October 1, 2009, http://www.chicagoreader.com/Bleader/archives/2009 /10/01/home-fires.

84 **"Saturday 17th Sunned, read, biked"** Richard Burton, diary entry, May 1975, *The Richard Burton Diaries* (New Haven, CT: Yale University Press, 2012), 595.

84–85 **"The events in our lives"** Eudora Welty, *One Writer's Beginnings* (Boston: Harvard University Press, 1995), 68–69.

85 **"The blizzard doesn't last forever"** Ray Bradbury, essay in *Snoopy's Guide to the Writing Life*, ed. Barnaby Conrad and Monte Schulz (New York: Writer's Digest Books, 2002), 162.

85 **"POZZO [*suddenly furious*]"** Samuel Beckett, *Waiting for Godot: Tragicomedy in 2 Acts* (New York: Grove, 1954). 109.

85–86 **"For only you could watch yourself"** John Ashbery, "The Bungalows," in *Selected Poems* (New York: Viking, 1985), 116.

86 **"With alcohol it was decompression"** Robin Williams, interview by Bill Zehme, "Robin Williams: The Rolling Stone Interview," *Rolling Stone*, February 25, 2009, http://www.rollingstone.com/movies/features/robin-williams -the-rolling-stone-interview-19880225.

86 **"What wound did ever heal"** William Shakespeare, *Othello*, in *The Riverside Shakespeare*, 2nd ed. (Boston: Houghton Mifflin, 1997), 2:1267.

86 **"The solution is not to suppress"** Lama Thubten Yeshe, *Introduction to Trantra: The Transformation of Desire* (Somerville, MA: Wisdom Publications, 2014), 74.

87 **"For me there was a real repulsion"** David Foster Wallace, interview by Laura Miller, *Salon*, March 9, 1996, http://www.salon.com/1996/03/09 /wallace_5/.

87 **"Sign on to a process"** Chuck Close on "Note to Self" series, CBS *This Morning*, producer Paige Kendig, April 10, 2012.

87 **"In a dark time"** Theodore Roethke, "In a Dark Time," in *The Collected Poems of Theodore Roethke* (New York: Anchor Press/Doubleday, 1975), 231.

88   **"The brave are patient"** Louise Glück, "From the Japanese," in *Poems 1962–2012* (New York: Farrar, Straus and Giroux, 2012), 195.

88   **"Let everything happen"** Rainer Maria Rilke, "The Book of Hours," in *The Poetry of Rilke*, trans. and ed. Edward Snow (New York: North Point Press, 2009), 33.

88   **"Be of good hope"** May Sarton, letter to Madeleine L'Engle, in *May Sarton: Selected Letters, 1916–1954*, ed. by Susan Sherman (New York: W. W. Norton, 1997), 351.

88   **"There are mountainous, arduous days"** Marcel Proust, *Remembrance of Things Past*, vol. 1: *Swann's Way*, trans. C. K. Scott Moncrieff and Terence Kilmartin (New York: Random House, 1981), 424.

88–89 **"I keep crying out"** Seneca, Epistle 27, in *Epistles: 1–65*, trans. Richard M. Gummere (Boston: Harvard University Press, 1917), 193.

89   **"Time will say nothing"** W. H. Auden, "If I Could Tell You," in *Collected Poems*, ed. by Edward Mendelson (New York: Random House, 2007), 312.

89   **"Longevity is more fun than the drugs"** Steve Van Zandt, interview by David Remnick, "We Are Alive," *New Yorker*, July 30, 2012, http://www .newyorker.com/magazine/2012/07/30/we-are-alive.

89   **"The first three or four months"** Jason Isbell, interview by Michael Bialas, "Hangout and About, Part 1: Jason Isbell Is Solo, But Not Alone," *Huffington Post*, May 3, 2013, http://www.huffingtonpost.com/michael-bialas/hangout -and-about-part-1_b_3205051.html.

89   **"So, a full year is coming"** Robert Lowell, letter to Elizabeth Bishop, in *Words in Air: The Complete Correspondence between Elizabeth Bishop and Robert Lowell*, ed. Thomas Travisano with Saskia Hamilton (New York: Farrar, Straus and Giroux, 2008), 503.

90   **"To have a problem"** Tennessee Williams, *Memoirs* (Garden City, NY: Doubleday, 1975), 3.

90   **"There's something about sober living"** Caroline Knapp, *Drinking: A Love Story* (New York: Dial Press, Random House, 2005), 108.

90   **"It was a weekday afternoon"** Billy Collins, "Scotland," in *Sailing Alone around the Room: New and Selected Poems* (New York: Random House, 2001), 166.

91   **"I miss drinking"** John Cheever, *The Journals of John Cheever* (New York: Knopf, 2011), 365.

91   **"It was humid in here"** Stephen King, *The Shining* (New York: Anchor Books, Random House, 2012), 25.

91–92 **"It is time now"** Mary Oliver, "Swimming, One Day in August," in *Red Bird* (Boston: Beacon Press, 2008), 56.

92–93 **"Master of beauty"** John Berryman, "Eleven Addresses to the Lord," in *John Berryman: Collected Poems, 1937–1971*, ed. By Charles Thornbury (New York: Farrar, Straus and Giroux, 2014), 215–21.

93–94 **"Shall we say"** Plato, *The Republic*, trans. G. M. A. Grube (Indianapolis: Hackett, 1974), 103.

94 **"a man that drinks"** Tennessee Williams, *Three Players of a Summer Game: And Other Stories* (London: Secker and Warburg, 1960), 17.

94 **"pride and drug addiction"** Stanley Crouch, *Kansas City Lightening: The Rise and Times of Charlie Parker* (New York: Harper, 2013), 229.

94–95 **"Many dubious and troublesome things"** Francesco Petrarch, "The Ascent of Mont Ventoux," trans. Hans Nachod, in *The Renaissance Philosophy of Man*, ed. Ernst Cassirer et al. (Chicago: Phoenix Books, University of Chicago Press, 1948), 42–43.

95 **"I am being driven forward"** Dag Hammarskjöld, "Thus it was," in *Markings*, trans. Leif Sjöberg and W. H. Auden (New York: Knopf, 1964), 5.

96 **"To bear is to conquer our fate"** Thomas Campbell, "Lines Written on Visiting a Scene in Argyleshire," in *Poems of Thomas Campbell* (London: Macmillan, 1904), 64.

96 **"Call up your courage again"** Virgil, *The Aeneid*, trans. Robert Fagles (New York: Penguin, 2006), 54.

96 **"...unfortunately, it's true:"** Charles Yu, *How to Live Safely in a Science Fictional Universe: A Novel* (New York: Pantheon, 2010), 54.

97 **"The past is gone"** Jim Jarmusch, *Broken Flowers*, directed by Jim Jarmusch (Universal Studios, DVD Focus Features, Los Angeles, 2006).

97 **"It is sometimes so bitterly cold"** Vincent van Gogh, letter to his brother Theo, in *The Letters of Vincent van Gogh*, trans. Arnold Pomerans (New York: Penguin, 1996), 63–64.

97 **"Enormous or not, life is made"** Vincent Hepp, quoted in May Sarton, *The House by the Sea: A Journal* (New York: Norton, 1977), 174.

97 **"Who knows what the day"** William Maxwell, letter to Eudora Welty, in *What There Is to Say, We Have Said: The Correspondence of Eudora Welty and William Maxwell*, ed. Suzanne Marrs (Boston: Houghton Mifflin, 2011), 213.

CHAPTER SIX

100 **"For every man must"** Fyodor Dostoevsky, *Crime and Punishment*, trans. Constance Black Garnett (New York: Modern Library, 1994), 17.

101 **"Do you know, sir"** Ibid., 18.

101 **"Do you understand, sir"** Ibid., 16.

101 **"You know every man"** Ibid., 18.

102 **"1. We admitted we were powerless"** *Alcoholics Anonymous*, 4th ed. (New York: Alcoholics Anonymous World Services, 2001), 354.

104 **"He had most likely acquired"** Fyodor Dostoevsky, *Crime and Punishment*, 16.

105 **"All that is secret"** Ibid., 17.

106 **"They say if you get far enough"** Tom Waits, "Blind Love," on *Rain Dogs* (Island Records, 1985).

106 **"It may be that"** Wendell Berry, "Marriage, Too, May Have Something to Teach Us," *Yoga Journal*, May–June 1987, 39.

106 **"Think of it like a date"** Dr. Keith Humphreys, quoted in David Sheff, *Clean: Overcoming Addiction and Ending America's Greatest Tragedy* (New York: Houghton Mifflin Harcourt, 2013), 149.

106–7 **"But is waiting forever"** Louise Glück, "Moonless Night," in *Poems 1962–2012* (New York: Farrar, Straus and Giroux, 2012), 313.

107 **"My father had always been wary"** Benjamin Cheever, *The Letters of John Cheever*, ed. Benjamin Cheever (New York: Simon and Schuster, 1988), 310.

107 **"From a certain point on"** Franz Kafka, *The Zürau Aphorisms of Franz Kafka*, trans. Michael Hofmann (New York: Schocken Books, 2006), 7.

107–8 **"The Texas beauties"** Domenica Ruta, *With or Without You* (New York: Spiegel & Grau, 2013), 169–71.

109 **"meanwhile in my head"** Anne Sexton, "Little Red Riding Hood," in *Transformations* (Boston: Houghton Mifflin, 2001), 75.

109–10 **"To be confirmed"** John Cheever, Berg Collection Papers, New York Public Library, quoted in Olivia Laing, *The Trip to Echo Spring: On Writers and Drinking* (New York: Picador, 2013), 267.

110 **"There was fear involved"** Caryl Pagel, "Telephone," *Iowa Review*, vol. 43, no. 2 (Fall 2013).

110 **"But nothing disturbs the feeling"** Jonathan Franzen, *Freedom: A Novel* (New York: Farrar, Straus and Giroux, 2010), 444.

111 **"lost among"** Franz Kafka, diary entry, in *Diaries: 1910–1923*, ed. Max Brod (New York: Schocken Books, 1976), 204.

111 **"And I myself"** Dante Alighieri, *The Inferno*, trans. W. P. Wilkie (Edinburgh: Edmonston and Douglas, 1862), 20.

111 **"It was terrifying"** Sacha Z. Scoblic, quoted in Amy Sullivan, "Q&A: The Author of *Unwasted* Talks about Socializing Sober," *Time*, July 28, 2011.

111 **"Now that my ladder's gone"** W. B. Yeats, "The Circus Animals' Desertion," in *The Collected Works of W. B. Yeats*, vol. 1: *The Poems*, ed. Richard J. Finneran (New York: Simon and Schuster, 1997), 356.

112 **"The mind must"** Kay Ryan, "New Rooms," *Poetry*, July–August 2012.

112 **"I did not know"** Evelyn Waugh, letter to Harold Acton, 1929, in *The Letters of Evelyn Waugh*, ed. Mark Amory (London: Penguin Books, 1982), 39.

112 **"I want to tear myself"** Khaled Hosseini, *The Kite Runner* (New York: Riverhead, 2003), 345.

113 **"Don't pick up a drink or drug"** Russell Brand, "Russell Brand: My Life without Drugs," *Guardian* (London), March 9, 2013.

113 **"One day at a time"** Roddy Doyle, *Paula Spencer* (New York: Viking, 2006), 202.

113 **"Sometimes an abyss opens"** Tomas Tranströmer, "Answers to Letters," in *The Great Enigma: New Collected Poems*, trans. Robin Fulton (New York: New Directions, 2006), 167.

114–15 **"Fake it till you make it"** Thomas Lynch, "The Way We Are," in *Bodies in Motion and at Rest* (New York: Norton, 2000), 106–7.

115 **"Everyone thinks their own situation"** Jeanette Winterson, *Oranges Are Not the Only Fruit* (New York: Grove Press, 1985), 161.

115 **"Every man"** Leo Tolstoy, *Anna Karenina*, trans. Richard Pevear and Larissa Volokhonsky (New York: Penguin, 2001), 302.

115 **"We are disclosing animals"** David Rakoff, *Half Empty* (New York: Doubleday, 2010), 109.

115–16 **"The relentlessly confessional tone"** Mark Stevens and Annalyn Swan, *de Kooning: An American Master* (New York: Knopf, 2004), 568.

116 **"Everybody's story is the same"** Roger Ebert, "My Name Is Roger, and I'm an Alcoholic," *Roger Ebert's Journal* (blog), August 25, 2009, rogerebert.com, http://www.rogerebert.com/rogers-journal/my-name-is-roger-and-im-an -alcoholic.

116 **"Their reward for enduring"** J. K. Rowling, *The Casual Vacancy* (New York: Little, Brown, 2012), 8.

116 **"A.A. is the world's largest"** Clancy Martin, "The Drunk's Club," *Harper's Magazine*, January 2011, 34.

117 **"I telephoned my AA sponsor"** Dan Fante, *Mooch* (Edinburgh: Canongate, 2000), 8.

117–18 **"When we had reached"** Dante Alighieri, *Purgatorio*, trans. Jean Hollander and Robert Hollander (New York: Doubleday, 2003), 79.

118 **"The tasks that have been entrusted"** Rainer Maria Rilke, *A Year with Rilke: Daily Readings from the Best of Rainer Maria Rilke*, trans. Joanna Macy and Anita Barrows (New York: HarperOne, 2009), 18.

118–19 **"I will leave here soon"** Ben Zitsman, "Dispatches from Suspension," in *The Sandspur* (Winter Park, FL), March 21, 2013.

119 **"A few months after I returned"** Richard Hell, *I Dreamed I Was a Very Clean Tramp: An Autobiography* (New York: HarperCollins, 2013), 282.

119 **"All I wanted to do"** Anne Lamott, *Operating Instructions* (New York: Pantheon, 1993), 227–28.

120 **"I used to be a boozer"** Willem de Kooning, quoted in Susan Murphy, "de Kooning and Me," *Huffington Post*, November 3, 2011.

120 **"God bless the busted boat"** Jason Isbell, "New South Wales," on *South-eastern* (Southeastern Records, 2013).

120 **"Suddenly the cherries were there"** Günter Grass, "Transformation," in

In the Egg and Other Poems, trans. Michael Hamburger and Christopher Middleton (New York: Harcourt Brace Jovanovich, 1977), 29.

120 **"My wife insisted"** John Cheever, letter to Tanya Litvinov, in *The Letters of John Cheever*, ed. Benjamin Cheever (New York: Simon and Schuster, 1988), 317.

121 **"O wonder!"** William Shakespeare, "The Tempest," in *The Riverside Shakespeare*, 2nd ed. (Boston: Houghton Mifflin, 1997), 2:1684.

121 **"How you doing, honey?"** Domenica Ruta, *With or Without You* (New York: Spiegel & Grau, 2013), 206.

121 **"You're on a pleasant cloud"** Floyd Patterson, quoted in David Remnick, *King of the World* (New York: Random House, 1998), 33.

122–23 **"when he realized"** David Foster Wallace, *Infinite Jest* (New York: Back Bay Books, 2006), 349–50.

123–24 **"At the end of every meeting"** Ruta, *With or Without You*, 189–90.

124 **"It says in the program"** Stephen King, interview by Christopher Lehmann-Haupt and Nathaniel Rich, "The Art of Fiction No. 189," *Paris Review*, no. 178 (Fall 2006).

124 **"The God thing"** Lennard Davis, quoted by David Sheff, *Clean* (New York: Houghton Mifflin Harcourt, 2013), 216.

124–25 **"You ask me how to pray"** Czeslaw Milosz, "On Prayer," in *Unattainable Earth*, trans. Robert Hass (New York: Ecco, 1986), 80.

125 **"And almost every one"** Arthur Hugh Clough, "Dipsychus," in *Arthur Hugh Clough: A Monograph*, by Samuel Waddington (London: George Bell and Sons, 1883), 232.

125 **"When he kneels"** Wallace, *Infinite Jest*, 443.

125 **"You know who my gods are"** Maurice Sendak, interview by Terry Gross, "Fresh Air Remembers Author Maurice Sendak," *Fresh Air*, National Public Radio, May 8, 2012.

126 **"In many ways"** Susan Cheever, *My Name Is Bill: Bill Wilson—His Life and the Creation of Alcoholics Anonymous* (New York: Simon and Schuster, 2005), 122.

126 **"In truth, Serenus"** Seneca, *Moral Essays*, trans. John W. Basore, Loeb Classical Library (Cambridge, MA: Harvard University Press, 1932), 2:213.

127 **"What I've learned"** Thomas Lynch, "The Way We Are," in *Bodies in Motion and at Rest* (New York: Norton, 2000), 112.

127 **"... I don't go to the meetings"** Ozzy Osbourne, *I Am Ozzy* (New York: Grand Central Publishing, 2011), 385.

127 **"For a lot of folks"** Jason Isbell, interview by Terry Gross, "Jason Isbell Locates His Musical Compass on 'Southeastern,'" *Fresh Air*, National Public Radio, July 17, 2013.

128 **"One day, I decided to attend"** Joe Queenan, *Closing Time* (New York: Viking, 2009), 306–7.

128 **"However many people AA helps"** David Sheff, *Clean: Overcoming Addiction and Ending America's Greatest Tragedy* (New York: Houghton Mifflin Harcourt, 2013), 230.

129 **"Many people in AA"** Susan Cheever, "Is It Time to Take the Anonymous out of AA?" TheFix.com, April 7, 2011, http://www.thefix.com/content /breaking-rule-anonymity-aa.

129 **"It seems crazy"** Molly Jong-Fast, quoted in David Colman, "Challenging the Second 'A' in A.A.," *New York Times*, May 6, 2011.

129 **"While a few things change"** Ruta, *With or Without You*, 206.

CHAPTER SEVEN

132 **"I remember once"** Jill Faulkner Summers, quoted in *William Faulkner, a Life on Paper: A Transcription from the Movie Produced by the Mississippi Center for Educational Television*, script by A. I. Bezzerides (Jackson: University Press of Mississippi in cooperation with the Mississippi Authority for Educational Television, 1980), 92.

136 **"Home is the place"** Robert Frost, "Death of the Hired Hand," in *North of Boston* (New York: Henry Holt, 1914), 20.

137 **"The whiskey on your breath"** Theodore Roethke, "My Papa's Waltz," in *The Collected Poems of Theodore Roethke* (New York: Anchor Press/Doubleday, 1975), 43.

137–38 **"I never suspected"** Susan J. Miller, "Never Let Me Down," *Granta*, no. 47 (Spring 1994), 124.

138 **"I spent a lot of time"** Joe Queenan, *Closing Time* (New York: Viking, 2009), 74.

139 **"On afternoons"** Scott Russell Sanders, "Under the Influence," in *Earth Works: Selected Essays* (Bloomington: Indiana University Press, 2012), 59–60.

139–40 **"S E Y M O U R : What do you guys want"** Simon Rich, "Slumber Party," in *Ant Farm: And Other Desperate Situations* (New York: Random House, 2007), 40–41.

140–41 **"Mother is drinking"** Lynn Emanuel, "Frying Trout while Drunk," in *The Dig and Hotel Fiesta: Two Volumes of Poetry by Lynn Emanuel* (Urbana: University of Illinois Press, 1995), 79.

141 **"Drinking to handle"** Mary Karr, *Lit* (New York: HarperCollins, 2009), 108–09.

142 **"The mice's preference"** Stephen Braun, *Buzz: The Science and Lore of Alcohol and Caffeine* (New York: Oxford University Press, 1996), 90.

142–43 **"My father was not"** Geoffrey Wolff, *A Day at the Beach: Recollections* (New York: Alfred A. Knopf, 1992), 95–96.

143 **"Billy's ROTC uniform"** Todd DePastino, *Bill Mauldin: A Life Up Front* (New York: W. W. Norton, 2008), 36–37.

144 **"It is difficult to feel"** Russell Brand, "Russell Brand: My Life without Drugs," *Guardian* (London), March 9, 2013.

144 **"The last I see"** Ken Kesey, *One Flew over the Cuckoo's Nest* (New York: Penguin, 2002), 189.

144–45 **"you are the loch ness monster"** Jeffrey McDaniel, "Zugzwang," in *The Endarkenment* (Pittsburgh, PA: University of Pittsburgh Press, 2008), 15.

145 **"The handwriting on the wall"** Stephen King, *The Shining* (New York: Anchor Books, 2012), 73–74.

145 **"The house rocked"** Raymond Carver, "From the East, Light," in *All of Us: The Collected Poems* (New York: Alfred A. Knopf, 1998), 168.

146 **"It takes so little"** Milan Kundera, *The Book of Laughter and Forgetting*, trans. Michael Henry Heim (New York: Penguin, 1980), 206–7.

146 **"If someone says"** Ivan Chermayeff, quoted in Alice Rawsthorn, "The Man Who Broke the Record on 'Let It Bleed,'" *New York Times*, December 11, 2011.

146 **"Nothing was ever said"** Adela Rogers St. Johns, *Final Verdict* (New York: Doubleday, 1962), 358.

146 **"I didn't want to hear"** Betty Ford with Chris Chase, *Betty: A Glad Awakening* (New York: Doubleday, 1987), 7.

147 **"Did you say Sebastian"** Evelyn Waugh, *Brideshead Revisited* (New York: Back Bay Books, 2012), 150.

147 **"wants my son"** Lucille Clifton, "white lady (a street name for cocaine)," in *The Collected Poems of Lucille Clifton: 1965–2010* (Rochester, NY: BOA Editions, 2012), 334–35.

147–48 **"I was no longer invited"** Seth Mnookin, "Harvard and Heroin," *Salon*, August 27, 1999.

148 **"*Maybe we shouldn't leave*"** Wendy Mnookin, "Relapse," in *To Get Here* (Rochester, NY: BOA Editions, 1999), 37.

148–49 **"MARY: [*Her eyes become fixed...*]"** Eugene O'Neill, *Long Day's Journey into Night* (New Haven, CT: Yale University Press, 1989), 70.

149 **"The predicament I found"** Queenan, *Closing Time*, 82.

149 **"I never knew him to lie"** Scott Russell Sanders, "Under the Influence," in *Earth Works: Selected Essays* (Bloomington: Indiana University Press, 2012), 58–59.

150 **"It's no good Charles"** Evelyn Waugh, *Brideshead Revisited* (New York: Back Bay Books, 2012), 161.

150 **"To be an addict"** David Carr, *The Night of the Gun: A Reporter Investigates the Darkest Story of His Life—His Own* (New York: Simon and Schuster, 2009), 15.

150 **"Marge, it takes two"** Matt Groening, "Colonel Homer," *The Simpsons*, March 26, 1992.

150 **"Friends and friends of friends"** David Sheff, *Beautiful Boy: A Father's Journey through His Son's Addiction* (Boston: Houghton Mifflin, 2008), 93.

151 **"It ain't a question"** James Baldwin, "Sonny's Blues," in *The Oxford Book of American Short Stories*, ed. Joyce Carol Oates (New York: Oxford University Press, 1992), 419.

151 **"My first resolve"** John Cheever, *The Journals of John Cheever* (New York: Knopf, 2011), 176.

151 **"That day at McLean's"** Seth Mnookin, "Harvard and Heroin," *Salon*, August 27, 1999.

152 **"DOROTHY: I'm frightened"** Noel Langley, Florence Ryerson, and Edgar Allan Woolf, *The Wizard of Oz* (Los Angeles: Metro-Goldwyn Mayer, 1939).

152–53 **"My father called to me"** Mary Oliver, "The Lake," in *No Voyage: And Other Poems* (Boston: Houghton Mifflin, 1965), 49–50.

153 **"Don't do anything"** Henry James, letter to Grace Norton, in *Henry James: Selected Letters*, ed. Leon Edel (Boston: Harvard University Press, 1987), 191.

154 **"you were in your twenties"** Robert Lowell, "Man and Wife," in *Selected Poems*, expanded ed. (New York: Farrar, Strauss and Giroux, 2006), 131.

154–55 **"by what logic"** Louise Glück, "Clover," in *Poems 1962–2012* (New York: Farrar, Straus and Giroux, 2012), 272.

155 **"I prayed ceaselessly"** Patti Smith, *Just Kids* (New York: Ecco, 2010), 275.

155 **"Seth didn't want me"** Wendy Mnookin, "My Son, the Junkie," *Salon*, August 27, 1999.

156 **"Her sister Marjorie"** Mark Stevens and Annalyn Swan, *de Kooning: An American Master* (New York: Knopf, 2004), 577–78.

156 **"SONYA: It's not like you!"** Anton Chekhov, *Chekhov: The Four Major Plays*, trans. Curt Columbus (Chicago: Ivan R. Dee, 2005), 113.

156–57 **"I threatened to leave"** Laila Nabulsi, quoted in Corey Seymour and Jann Wenner, *Gonzo: The Life of Hunter S. Thompson* (New York: Little, Brown, 2007), 242.

157 **"He was an alcoholic"** Jann Wenner, quoted in Corey Seymour and Jann Wenner, *Gonzo: The Life of Hunter S. Thompson* (New York: Little, Brown, 2007), 386.

157 **"His wife tried"** Deborah Solomon, *Jackson Pollock: A Biography* (New York: Cooper Square Press, 2001), 241.

158 **"In the turmoil"** Wendy Mnookin, "My Son, the Junkie."

158 **"You're gonna have"** Beth Nielsen Chapman, "Save Yourself," recorded by Suzy Bogguss on *Aces* (EMI, 1991).

158 **"I can't save myself"** Tennessee Williams, notebook entry, *Tennessee Williams: Notebooks*, ed. Margaret Bradham Thornton (New Haven, CT: Yale University Press, 2006), 203.

159 **"According to Elaine"** Stevens and Swan, *de Kooning*, 565.

159 **"I remember getting"** David Markson, interview by Joseph Tabbi, "A Conversation with David Markson," *Review of Contemporary Fiction*, vol. 10, no. 2 (Summer 1990).

160–61 **"My wife's younger brother"** Philip Schultz, "My Wife," in *Failure: Poems* (New York: Houghton Mifflin Harcourt, 2009), 25–26.

161 **"I longed for someone"** Sheff, *Beautiful Boy*, 241.

161–62 **"When I saw you outside"** Jeffrey McDaniel, "Oblivion Chiclets," in *The Endarkenment* (Pittsburgh, PA: University of Pittsburgh Press, 2008), 60.

163 **"In this country"** Billie Holiday with William Dufty, *Lady Sings the Blues* (New York: Penguin, 1984), 188.

163 **"Anyone who has lived"** Sheff, *Beautiful Boy*, 13.

163 **"My wife, a former Al-Anon junkie"** Clancy Martin, "The Drunk's Club: A.A., the Cult That Cures," *Harper's Magazine*, January 2011, 38.

163–64 **"Joey, I know"** Queenan, *Closing Time*, 305.

164–65 **"One of the few upsides"** Dax Shepard, "My Father's Horniness," *Don't Try* (blog), March 20, 2013, http://daxtumbler.tumblr.com/post/45876994574/my-fathers-horniness.

165 **"I cheated three"** John Phillips, *Papa John* (Garden City, NY: Doubleday, 1986), 427.

165–66 **"The Redskins are winning"** Adrian C. Louis, "The Fine Printing on the Label of a Bottle of Non-alcohol Beer," in *Vortex of Indian Fevers* (Evanston, IL: Northwestern University Press, 1995), 44–45.

167 **"But I should dishonor"** Chief Simon Pokagon, "Chief Pokagon Speech in Angola" (August 16, 1894), Steuben County Indiana: Through the Years, April 1, 2010, http://steubenindianahistory.blogspot.com/2010/04/chief-pokagon-speech-in-angola.html.

167–68 **"I am grateful"** Mnookin, "My Son, the Junkie."

168 **"When [my father] went into rehab"** Susan Cheever, interview by Krista Tippett, "The Spirituality of Addiction and Recovery," *On Being*, American Public Media, May 15, 2008.

168–69 **"Our annual birthday"** John Updike, "Endpoint," in *Endpoint and Other Poems* (New York: Knopf, 2009), 19–20.

169 **"In August, 1988"** Miller, "Never Let Me Down," 132–33.

170 **"That is how the story ends"** Scott Russell Sanders, "Under the Influence," 56.

170 **"You are past love"** Thomas Hardy, "Your Last Drive," in *Hardy: Selected Poems*, ed. Robert Mezey (New York: Penguin, 1998), 81.

170 **"I hold a five-year diary"** Anne Sexton, "All My Pretty Ones," in *The Complete Poems: Anne Sexton* (New York: Mariner Books, 1999), 51.

170–71 **"People do what they can"** James McAuley, "Because," in *Collected Poems, 1936–1970* (Sydney: Angus & Robertson, 1994), 47.

171 **"I wondered if that"** Khaled Hosseini, *The Kite Runner* (New York: Riverhead, 2003), 359.

171 **"(*In my sleep I dreamed this poem*)"** Mary Oliver, "The Uses of Sorrow," in *Thirst: Poems* (Boston: Beacon Press, 2007), 52.

CHAPTER EIGHT

174 "...and so to the pewterers" Samuel Pepys, diary entry, in *The Diary of Samuel Pepys*, vol. 3: *1662*, ed. by Robert Latham and William Matthews (Berkeley: University of California Press, 1971), 41.

175 **"And so to supper"** Ibid., 3:50.

175 **"scandalously overserved with drink"** Henry Whitley, *Samuel Pepys and the World He Lived In* (London: Bickers and Sons, 1880), 5.

177 **"That nobody who's ever gotten"** David Foster Wallace, *Infinite Jest* (New York: Back Bay Books, 2006), 204.

178 **"Thence to dinner"** Pepys, diary entry, in *The Diary of Samuel Pepys*, 3:107.

179 **"To forget the world's abundance"** Robert M. Coates and E. B. White, "Notes and Comment," *New Yorker*, November 29, 1952, 31.

179 **"Those venal and furtive loves"** James Joyce, "A Painful Case," in *Dubliners* (New York: Penguin, 1976), 97.

179 **"But when he was cured"** Horace, *The Epistles of Horace*, trans. David Ferry (New York: Farrar, Straus and Giroux, 2002), 143.

179 **"Now that I am cured"** Jean Cocteau, *Opium: The Diary of a Cure*, trans. Margaret Crosland and Sinclair Road (New York: Grove Press, 1958), 146.

180 **"Johnson observed"** James Boswell, *The Life of Samuel Johnson, LL.D.* (New York: Heritage Press, 1963), 2:171.

180 **"The most common outcome"** Walter Ling, "Detoxification," slide in "Opioid Dependence: Treatment Options," speech presented at Suboxone Advisory Board Meeting, Kaohsiung, Taiwan, November 4, 2007.

180 **"When you keep hearing"** Clancy Martin, "The Drunk's Club: A.A., the Cult That Cures," *Harper's*, January, 2011, 35.

180–81 **"After I had cut off my hands"** Denise Levertov, "Intrusion," in *Poems, 1968–1972* (New York: New Directions, 1988), 202.

181 **"the giant returns"** Robert Lax, "[the giant/returns]," in *Poems (1962–1997)* (Seattle: Wave Books, 2013), 125.

182 **"How came any reasonable being"** Thomas De Quincey, *Confessions of an English Opium-Eater* (New York, Penguin, 2003), 7.

182 **"'I did that,' says my memory"** Friedrich Nietzsche, *Beyond Good and Evil*, trans. Helen Zimmern (Rockville, MD: Serenity Publishers, 2008), 58.

182 **"What then, you ask, is an evil?"** Seneca, Epistle 85, in *Epistles: 66–92*, trans. Richard M. Gummere (Boston: Harvard University Press, 1917), 301.

182–83 **"Waves of despair"** Louise Glück, "Fable," in *Poems 1962–2012* (New York: Farrar, Straus and Giroux: 2012), 423.

183 **"Like love, like seasickness"** Cocteau, *Opium: The Diary of a Cure*, 57.

183–84 **"You do look a little ill"** Franz Wright, "Alcohol," in *Ill Lit: New and Selected Poems* (Oberlin, OH: Oberlin College Press, 1998), 38.

184   "The beauty of quitting" Jim Jarmusch, *Coffee and Cigarettes* (2003), directed by Jim Jarmusch (MGM DVD, Los Angeles, 2004).

184   "I AM DRINKING NOW" Spalding Gray, journal entry, in *The Journals of Spalding Gray* (New York: Knopf, 2011), 199.

185   "Captain Cock and I" Samuel Pepys, diary entry, in *The Diary of Samuel Pepys*, 3:31.

185   "And the burnt Fool's bandaged finger" Rudyard Kipling, "The Gods of the Copybook Headings," in *Kipling* (New York: Knopf, Everyman's Library, 2007), 233.

185   "The rat stops gnawing" Bernard DeVoto, *The Hour: A Cocktail Manifesto* (Portland, OR: Tin House Books, 2010), 125.

185   "Addiction is when you do the thing" Philip Seymour Hoffman, quoted by Jim Dwyer, "Lies about Hoffman Yield Prize for Playwrights," *New York Times*, February 26, 2014, A1.

186   "This was what always happened" Iris Murdoch, *Under the Net: A Comic Novel about Work and Love, Wealth and Fame* (New York: Penguin, 1977), 9.

186   "He told me I might now have the pleasure" Boswell, *The Life of Samuel Johnson L.L.D.*, 3:184.

186   "I fell off my disciplined waggon" Richard Burton, diary entry, September 29, 1969, in *The Richard Burton Diaries* (New Haven, CT: Yale University Press, 2012), 327.

187   "...a wineglassful won't make a man drunk" Anton Chekhov, letter to Madame M. V. Kiselyov, in *Letters of Anton Chekhov to His Family and Friends*, trans. Constance Garnett (New York: Macmillan, 1920), 56.

187   "I'm on the wagon" F. Scott Fitzgerald, quoted in Tony Buttita, *The Lost Summer: A Personal Memoir of F. Scott Fitzgerald* (New York: St. Martin's Press, 1987), 4.

187   "And as soon as the morning's work" Jack London, *John Barleycorn* (London: Mills & Boon, 1914), 268–69.

187   "The quaking of the solid ground" Thomas Mann and Herman George Scheffauer, *Early Sorrow* (New York: Knopf, 1930), 10.

188   "The guests tried to make sense" Deborah Solomon, *Jackson Pollock: A Biography* (New York: Cooper Square Press, 2001), 212.

188   "And thus the whirligig of time" William Shakespeare, "Twelfth Night," *The Riverside Shakespeare*, 2nd ed. (Boston: Houghton Mifflin, 1997), 1:473.

188   "The next day he is up" William Maxwell, *So Long, See You Tomorrow* (New York: Random House, 1989), 67–68.

188   "Not working is terribly painful" John Cheever, letter to William Maxwell, in *The Letters of John Cheever*, ed. Benjamin Cheever (New York: Simon and Schuster, 1988), 270.

188–89   "i was talking to a moth" Don Marquis, "the lesson of the moth," in *the lives and times of archy and mehitabel* (New York: Doubleday, 1950), 95–96.

191 **"His son Phelim"** Liam Collins, "The 'Grouchy' Dubliner Who Never Lost His Sense of Humour," *Independent*, August 17, 2008, http://www.indepen dent.ie/irish-news/the-grouchy-dubliner-who-never-lost-his-sense-of -humour-26469907.html.

191 **"Don't confront me"** Jackson Browne, "These Days," on *For Everyman* (Elektra, 1973).

191 **"Yes, he knew"** Rainer Maria Rilke, *The Notebooks of Malte Laurids Brigge*, trans. M. D. Herter Norton (New York: W. W. Norton, 1949), 51.

192 **"Having been so drunk yesterday"** Richard Burton, diary entry, in *The Richard Burton Diaries* (New Haven, CT: Yale University Press, 2012), 609.

192 **"She had firm faith"** Evelyn Waugh, *Brideshead Revisited* (New York: Little Brown, 2012), 265.

192 **"Morals first gave way"** Livy, *History of Rome*, bks. 1–2, trans. B. O. Foster (Boston: Harvard University Press, 1919), 7.

192–93 **"Why are you drinking?"** Antoine de Saint-Exupéry, *The Little Prince*, trans. Richard Howard (New York: Houghton Mifflin Harcourt, 2000), 51.

193 **"For the shoe pinches"** John Ashbery, "The Ecclesiast," in *Selected Poems* (New York: Viking, 1985), 59.

193 **"I have by a late oath"** Pepys, diary entry, in *The Diary of Samuel Pepys*, 3:98.

193 **"But how can one be happy"** Seneca, Epistle 85, in *Epistles: 66–92*, 297.

193 **"Drank a cup of ale"** Pepys, diary entry, in *The Diary of Samuel Pepys*, 3:196–97.

194 **"We are lost"** Dante Aligheri, *The Inferno of Dante*, trans. Robert Pinsky (New York: Farrar, Straus and Giroux, 1994), 37.

194 **"Man is stupefied"** Giacomo Leopardi, *Zibaldone* (New York: Farrar, Straus and Giroux, 2013), 2071.

194 **"He who seeks to approach"** Walter Benjamin, "Excavation and Memory," in *Selected Writings*, vol. 2, pt. 2: *1931–1934*, ed. Michael W. Jennings, Howard Eiland, and Gary Smith, and trans. Rodney Livingstone et al. (Cambridge, MA: Harvard University Press, 1999), 576.

195 **"The truth is he with kindness"** Pepys, diary entry, in *The Diary of Samuel Pepys*, 3:199–200.

195 **"This day my oaths for drinking"** Ibid., diary entry, 3:207.

195 **"Strange to see how easily"** Ibid., diary entry, in 3:209.

196 **"He saw that all the struggles"** Jack Kerouac, *The Town and the City* (New York: Harcourt, Brace, 1970), 472.

196 **"Let all such fancies"** Samuel Johnson, in Boswell, *The Life of Samuel Johnson LL.D.*, 1:337–38.

197 **"Of all the pitfalls"** Agnes Martin, *Writings* (New York: Distributed Art Publishers, 1993), 73.

197–98 **"Left off the highway"** Raymond Carver, "Waiting," in *All of Us: The Collected Poems* (New York: Vintage, 2000), 205.

198 **"Okay. Start over"** John Berryman, *Recovery* (New York: Farrar, Straus and Giroux, 1973), 8.

198 **"MARGE: I'm sorry Maggie"** Bill Odenkirk, "Crook and Ladder," *The Simpsons*, May 6, 2007.

198–99 **"My second visit to Hazelden"** Eric Clapton, *Clapton: The Autobiography* (New York: Doubleday, 2007), 234.

199–200 **"When I arrived at Silver Hill Hospital"** Nile Rodgers, *Le Freak: An Upside Down Story of Family, Disco and Destiny* (New York: Random House, 2011), 271.

200 **"The last of man's great unchained beasts"** Michael Timmins, "Mariner's Song," on *Caution Horses* (Universal Musical Publishing Group, 1990).

200 **"The path up there is so steep"** Albert Camus, *Notebooks, 1935–1951* (New York: Marlowe, 1965), 31.

200 **"But, however, as soon as I came home"** Pepys, diary entry, in *The Diary of Samuel Pepys*, 3:230.

CHAPTER NINE

202 **"No other word will do"** Raymond Carver, "Gravy," in *All of Us: The Collected Poems* (New York: Vintage, 2000), 292.

203 **"Instead of dying from alcohol"** Tess Gallagher, "Instead of Dying," lecture presented at Academi Intoxication Conference, Llandudno, Wales, February 24, 2006.

203 **"I'm prouder of that"** Raymond Carver, interview by Mona Simpson and Lewis Buzbee, "The Art of Fiction No. 76," *Paris Review*, no. 88 (Summer 1983), http://www.theparisreview.org/interviews/3059/the-art-of-fiction -no-76-raymond-carver.

206 **"The world is all gates"** Ralph Waldo Emerson, *Prose Works of Ralph Waldo Emerson*, vol. 3 (Boston: Houghton, Osgood and Co., 1880), 267.

207 **"What matters most is"** Charles Bukowski, "how is your heart?" in *The Pleasures of the Damned: Poems, 1951–1993* (New York: Ecco, 2008), 512–513.

207–8 **"The deed took all my heart"** Mary Oliver, "The Return," in *No Voyage and Other Poems* (Boston: HoughtonMifflin, 1965), 62–63.

209 **"We know it is close"** Kay Ryan, "Relief," in *The Best of It: New and Selected Poems* (New York: Grove Press, 2011), 134.

209 **"As painful as my addictions have been"** Sid Caesar, *Caesar's Hours: My Life in Comedy with Love and Laughter* (New York: PublicAffairs, 2003), 270.

210 **"My holy of holies"** Anton Chekhov, letter to Alexis Pleshcheev, in *Letters of Anton Chekhov to His Family and Friends*, trans. Constance Garnett (New York: Macmillan, 1920), 38.

210 **"The life back then is gone"** Carver, interview by Simpson and Buzbee, "The Art of Fiction No. 76."

210 **"He must not doubt about it"** Samuel Johnson, in James Boswell, *The Life of Samuel Johnson, LL.D* (New York: Heritage Press, 1963), 2:458.

210 **"The pain was like burning"** Austin Grossman, *Soon I Will Be Invincible* (New York: Pantheon, 2007), 128.

211 **"I learned very early"** Chuck Close on "Note to Self" series, *CBS This Morning*, producer Paige Kendig, April 10, 2012.

211 **"You have those memories"** Edie Falco, interview by Kevin Sessums, "Edie Falco Comes Clean," *Daily Beast*, May 5, 2010, http://www.thedailybeast.com/articles/2010/05/16/edie-falco-comes-clean.html.

211 **"Listen: there's a hell"** E. E. Cummings, "pity this monster, manunkind," in *100 Selected Poems* (New York: Grove, 1994), 89.

211–12 **"'Carpe diem' doesn't mean"** Nicholson Baker, *The Anthologist: A Novel* (New York: Simon and Schuster, 2009), 127.

212 **"The key factor is the environment"** Carl Hart, quoted in John Tierney, "Tracing Addiction Outside the Brain," *New York Times*, September 17, 2013, D3.

212 **"The dead drug leaves a ghost"** Jean Cocteau, *Opium: The Diary of a Cure*, trans. Margaret Crosland and Sinclair Road (New York: Grove Press, 1958), 74.

212–13 **"Thus, when reading in my deck-chair"** Jack London, *John Barleycorn* (London: Mills & Boon, 1914), 206–7.

213 **"A few days later"** John F. Murray, "O'Phelan Drinking," *New Yorker*, October 30, 1977, 44.

213 **"A man should cultivate his mind"** Samuel Johnson, in Boswell, *The Life of Johnson LL.D.*, 3:33.

214 **"your life is your life"** Charles Bukowski, "the laughing heart," in *Betting on the Muse: Poems and Stories* (Santa Rosa, CA: Black Sparrow Press, 1994), 400.

215 **"You can't really be too concerned"** Tom Waits, quoted in Barney Hoskyns, *Lowside of the Road: A Life of Tom Waits* (London: Faber and Faber, 2009), xii.

215 **"Life, although it may only be"** Mary Shelley, *Frankenstein* (New York: Penguin, 2003), 102.

215 **"I don't know Who"** Dag Hammarskjöld, *Markings*, trans. Leif Sjöberg and W. H. Auden (New York: Knopf, 1964), 205.

216 **"The world is a fine place"** Ernest Hemingway, *For Whom the Bell Tolls* (New York: Scribner, 1940), 490.

216 **"The mind is malleable"** Matthieu Ricard, quoted in Anthony Barnes, "The Happiest Man in the World?" *Independent* (London), January 21, 2007.

216–17 **"Sometimes I wish I were still out"** Tony Hoagland, "Jet," in *Donkey Gospel* (St. Paul: Graywolf Press, 1998), 3.

217–18 **"it's good not to drink"** Maureen N. McLane, "Every Day a Shiny Bright New Day," *Poetry*, September 2013, http://www.poetryfoundation.org /poetrymagazine/poem/246314.

218 **"I have many fond memories"** Richard Hell, *I Dreamed I Was a Very Clean Tramp: An Autobiography* (New York: HarperCollins, 2013), 251.

218 **"It's better to burn out"** Neil Young and Jeff Blackburn, "My My, Hey Hey (Out of the Blue)," recorded by Neil Young and Crazy Horse on *Rust Never Sleeps* (Reprise, 1979).

219 **"It's better to fade away"** John Lennon, quoted in David Sheff *All We Are Saying: The Last Major Interview with John Lennon and Yoko Ono* (New York: St. Martin's, 2000), 57.

219 **"Through loyalty to the past"** André Gide, journal entry, in *The Journals of André Gide*, vol. 2: *1928–1939*, trans. Justin O'Brien (Urbana: University of Illinois Press, 2000), 31.

219 **"Not drinking is no easy passport"** Upton Sinclair, *The Cup of Fury* (Manhasset, NY: Channel Press, 1956), 174.

219 **"I urge you to please notice"** Kurt Vonnegut, *A Man without a Country* (New York: Random House, 2007), 132.

220 **"won't you celebrate with me"** Lucille Clifton, "won't you celebrate with me," in *The Book of Light* (Port Townsend, WA: Copper Canyon Press, 1993), 25.

220–21 **"Looking out over"** John Ashbery, "The Skaters," in *Collected Poems 1956–1987*, ed. Mark Ford (New York: Library of America, 2008), 73.

221 **"JOHNSON: No, Sir, wine gives not light"** Samuel Johnson, in Boswell, *The Life of Samuel Johnson, L.L.D.*, 2:288.

221 **"You think when you wake up"** Cormac McCarthy, *No Country for Old Men* (New York: Random House, 2005), 227.

222 **"Imagine you wake up"** Rita Dove, "Dawn Revisited," in *On the Bus with Rosa Parks: Poems* (New York: Norton, 1999), 36.

222 **"There isn't a soul on earth"** Billie Holiday with William Dufty, *Lady Sings the Blues* (New York: Penguin, 1984), 189.

222 **"I caution you as I was never cautioned"** Louise Glück, "The Sensual World," in *Poems 1962–2012*, 421.

223 **"So with men's dispositions"** Seneca, Epistle 52, in *Epistles: 1–65*, trans. Richard M. Gummere (Boston: Harvard University Press, 1917), 347.

223 **"Part of the process of recovering"** Jack London, *John Barleycorn* (London: Mills & Boon, 1914), 238.

223 **"Now there is one thing I can tell you"** Marcel Proust, quoted in Roland Barthes, *Mourning Diary* (New York: Hill and Wang, 2010), 170.

223 **"One of the secrets"** Iris Murdoch, *The Sea, the Sea* (New York: Penguin Books, 1980), 8.

224 **"Living beings, in turning a corner"** Takashi Hiraide, *The Guest Cat*, trans. Eric Selland (New York: New Directions, 2001), 20.

224 **"How we spend our days"** Annie Dillard, *The Writing Life* (New York: Harper Perennial, 1990), 32.

224 **"Sooner or later"** Bruce Springsteen, "Straight Time," on *The Ghost of Tom Joad* (Columbia Records, 1995).

225–26 **"I'm awake; I am in the world"** Louise Glück, "Stars," in *Poems 1962– 2012*, 425–26.

226 **"AUNT MAE: He knows a hero"** Alvin Sargent, *Spider-Man* 2 (Columbia Pictures, 2004).

227 **"Everything that happens"** Jorge Luis Borges, "Blindness," in *Selected Non-Fiction*, ed. Eliot Weinberger (New York: Penguin, 1999), 483.

227 **"We experience pain"** Marilynne Robinson, interview by Sarah Fay, "The Art of Fiction No. 198," *Paris Review*, no. 186 (Fall 2008), http://www.the parisreview.org/interviews/5863/the-art-of-fiction-no-198-marilynne -robinson.

227 **"You have been as brave as anybody"** Marlon Brando, quoted in Olivia Laing, *The Trip to Echo Spring: On Writers and Drinking* (New York: St. Martin's, 2013), 216.

227–28 **"...the Ryoan-ji rock garden in Kyoto"** Jane Hirshfield, "Thoreau's Hound: On Hiddenness," in *Ten Windows: How Great Poems Transform the World* (New York: Knopf, 2015), 94; first published in *American Poetry Review*, May–June 2002.

228 **"You have led me from my bondage"** Dante Aligheri, "Paradiso," canto 31, in *The Divine Comedy*, trans. John Ciardi (New York, Penguin NAL, 2003), 872.

228 **"I live soberly"** Vincent van Gogh, letter to his brother Theo, in *Dear Theo: The Autobiography of Vincent van Gogh*, ed. Irving Stone with Jean Stone (New York: Plume, 1995), 438.

228 **"A man goes far to find out"** Theodore Roethke, "In a Dark Time," in *The Collected Poems of Theodore Roethke* (New York: Anchor Press/Doubleday, 1975), 231.

228–29 **"As you set out for Ithaka"** Constantine P. Cavafy, "Ithaka," in *Collected Poems*, trans. Edmund Keeley and Philip Sherrard and ed. George Savidis, rev. ed. (Princeton, NJ: Princeton University Press, 1992), 36–37.

230 **"'Kindness' covers all my political beliefs"** Roger Ebert, *Life Itself: A Memoir* (New York: Hachette, Grand Central Publishing, 2011), 414.

230 **"For us, there is only the trying"** T. S. Eliot, "East Coker," in *Collected Poems, 1909–1962* (New York: Harcourt Brace Jovanovich, 1991), 189.

230 **"Another opportunity was given"** Hammarskjöld, *Markings*, 158.

230–31 **"But what could you do?"** Elizabeth Strout, *Amy and Isabelle* (New York: Random House, Vintage, 1998), 284.

231 **"...I believe in intention and I believe in work"** Leslie Jamison, "The Empathy Exams" *Believer*, February 2014, http://www.believermag.com /issues/201402/?read=article_jamison.

231 **"The world breaks everyone"** Ernest Hemingway, *A Farewell to Arms* (New York: Scribner, 1997), 226.

231 **"And once the storm is over"** Haruki Murakami, *Kafka on the Shore*, trans. by Philip Gabriel (New York: Vintage, 2006), 6.

232 **"There's still time to change things"** Siri Hustvedt, *The Blazing World* (New York: Simon and Schuster, 2014), 17.

PERMISSIONS

INDEX